DEE WILLIAMS is a teacher and sustainability advocate. She is the co-owner of Portland Alternative Dwellings (www .padtinyhouses.com), where she leads workshops focused on tiny houses, green building, and community design. Her story has been featured on *Good Morning America* and *NBC Nightly News*, and on NPR, PBS, MSNBC, CNN, and CBC. She has also been profiled or featured in hundreds of online blogs and articles, and in print media including *Time*, the *New York Times*, and *Der Spiegel*. Williams lives in Olympia, Washington, with an overly ambitious Australian shepherd, in the shadow of the house of dear friends.

Praise for *The Big Tiny*

"[An] affecting memoir . . . Williams writes in *The Big Tiny* of finding a centeredness and peace in her little house, of being less fearful, more alive. Some of the best passages are when she describes the sensory experience of being inside: smelling raw cedar and knotty pine; listening to the weather."

—Steven Kurutz, *The New York Times*

"[N]o one makes the idea of living in a home the size of an area rug more appealing. . . . Williams's inspiring memoir will resonate with anyone on a quest to downsize, de-stress, let go, or feel at home. . . . An endearing, funny writer . . . [*The Big Tiny*] is a book as intimate and draw-you-in-close as Williams's little abode."   —Janet Eastman, *The Oregonian*

"[A] delightful encounter with the Tina Fey of the sustainability world, an empowered woman unafraid to admit she accidentally glued her hair to her house, as well as an incisive thinker on contemporary experience. . . . A hilarious and poignant memoir . . . Williams writes a down-to-earth manifesto for living life with intention and for geeking out, diving in, caring too deeply, and trying too hard in general."

—Mary Louise Schumacher, *Milwaukee Journal Sentinel*

"Williams has built an engaging and inspiring how-to/memoir that goes beyond the DIY perspective."   —*Booklist*

"*The Big Tiny* will find sympathy with readers frustrated with the conventional rat race."   —*Kirkus Reviews*

"In *The Big Tiny*, Dee Williams creates a portrait of humanity through her own compelling experience. That she has written about home and life with such humor and vulnerability, and in her own unique vernacular, makes her story all the more universal."

—Jay Shafer, author of *The Small House Book*

"*The Big Tiny* is irresistible. Dee Williams is as much fun on the page as she is in person. Comic, silly, and soulful, she takes us on her journey to simplify her life and along the way tunes in to our own inner desire to pare down to our nearly naked selves."

—Jim Lynch, author of
The Highest Tide and *Truth Like the Sun*

"*The Big Tiny* is a beautifully written narrative, one that goes beyond happiness and living simply. The power of Dee's words will touch your heart, make you laugh, cry, and change your life."

—Tammy Strobel, author of
You Can Buy Happiness (and It's Cheap)

"*The Big Tiny* is comedic, eloquent, and damn informative all at the same time. If Dee Williams's story hasn't inspired you to reevaluate your life already, this book just may be the swift kick in the pants you need—the final awakening blow all rolled into one biblio-burrito of badassness."

—Derek "Deek" Diedricksen,
HGTV host and honcho of Relaxshacks.com

"Dee Williams aims for happiness 85 percent of the time, but I think you'll be 100 percent happy with the wisdom she shares in this beautiful book."

—Chris Guillebeau, author of *The $100 Startup*

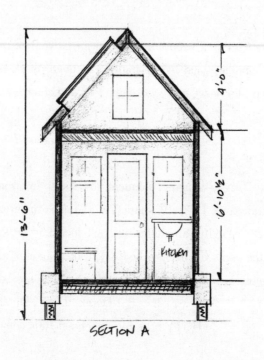

4'-0"

6'-10½"

13'-6"

Kitchen

SECTION A

The Big Tiny

A Built-It-Myself Memoir

DEE WILLIAMS

A PLUME BOOK

PLUME
Published by the Penguin Group
Penguin Group (USA) LLC
375 Hudson Street
New York, New York 10014

USA | Canada | UK | Ireland | Australia | New Zealand | India | South Africa | China
penguin.com
A Penguin Random House Company

First published in the United States of America by Blue Rider Press,
a member of Penguin Group (USA) LLC, 2014
First Plume Printing 2015

P REGISTERED TRADEMARK—MARCA REGISTRADA

THE LIBRARY OF CONGRESS HAS CATALOGED THE BLUE RIDER PRESS EDITION AS FOLLOWS:

Williams, Dee (Builder)
The big tiny : a built-it-myself memoir / Dee Williams.
p.   cm.
ISBN 978-0-399-16617-4 (hc.)
ISBN 978-0-14-218179-9 (pbk.)
1. Williams, Dee—Homes and haunts—United States.   2. Ecological houses—
United States—Design and construction.   3. Small houses—United States—Design
and construction.   4. Architects and builders—United States—Biography.
5. Do-it-yourself work—Social aspects—United States.   6. Alternative lifestyles—
United States.   7. Sustainable living—United States.   8. Olympia (Wash.)—
Biography.   9. Portland (Or.)—Biography.   I. Title.
TH4860.W525   2014   2014002151
640.92—dc23
[B]

Printed in the United States of America
5   7   9   10   8   6   4

Original hardcover design by Amanda Dewey

For Rita and RooDee

Contents

The Big Tiny

Happy Enough

For months now, I've been waking up at four in the morning. I've got this system down: I toss about in bed for a while, left to right, right to left, then lie flat on my back to stare into the knots in the wood ceiling. I watch my dog breathe as she sleeps, watch her legs jolt as she dreams of chasing rabbits. I look out the skylight window, watch the clouds and the moon; I stare at myself in the reflection of the window a few feet from my face, and wonder if I look as shadowy and pensive in real life as I do right now, a thought that causes me to make exaggerated sad-clown faces as in an old black-and-white movie—which cracks me up. I close my eyes and listen to my own whistling breath and I wonder if I have a vitamin deficiency, if I'm aging ungracefully or will die in the next half hour, which leads to the question of whether I'd want to be "found" in this position in these long johns with the elastic blown out at the waist, with dirty dishes in the sink, dog hair on the carpet, and a compost toilet full of pee. I rearrange myself, smooth out the blankets and uncrinkle my forehead, and think about the neighbors. I wonder if they are also awake and worrying about their vitamins.

Later, when I actually see the neighbors, I probably won't follow this line of questioning. Instead, I'll say something neutral like "S'up?" Or if there's more time, I'll bring up the clouds or the wind, or one of a thousand other things I've noticed floating around in the predawn backyard. I might describe the catfight in the alley or the way seagulls were cracking open clams by flying over and dropping them on the carport roof. I might not even mention that. People don't really want to hear about that kind of long-winded stuff when they casually ask "How you doing?" while they're dragging their rubbish bins out to the curb before driving off to work.

When I mentioned my early-morning waking to the old witch down the street, she explained that this is the time the "ceiling is the thinnest," the moment that the earth's creatures have the greatest access to the heavens; the time when nuns and priests wake to pray, shuffling in their prayer shawls and pouring themselves into the cosmos; the time the raccoons waddle down the alley into the nature preserve that is really just the woods behind the grade school; and the most common moment when people die. It is a magical time, or so she said.

Hearing all of that helped me feel less resentful about waking up so early, and now it seems less necessary to punch my pillow like bread dough. Instead, I wake up and I think about the day ahead or the day before, or I might try to decode a particular night sound—a porcupine or feral cats, a possum on the porch, or maybe college kids drunk and stumbling down the alley. I toss about until I can't stand it anymore, until I pitch everything to the side of the bed and carry my dog, RooDee, down the ladder, like she weighs twenty pounds instead of fifty, like this is what normal people do.

If the weather is good, I'll make a bit of tea and amble out onto the front porch to watch the sun crawl over the neighbor's garage. On the surface, it's nearly the same every time: I spend at least five minutes trying to make the dog's blanket (a hairy but warm apparatus) double as a seat cushion and a backrest, then I'll spend several minutes looking for my lost glasses, which I find on my head, and then I might notice that it's warmer today than yesterday.

If it's raining or cold outside (like it is all winter), I stay inside. I might jog in place while I brush my teeth, or I'll put on a hat and mittens while I light the cookstove. I've even gotten into the habit of warming my underthings by dangling them over the stove while I make coffee. I'm so comfortable with this work that I don't even see it as clever anymore, hardly worth mentioning except for the fact that I think I'm on to something: I've found a way to heat my bra without singeing the straps and to drape my long johns without lighting the kitchen shelves on fire. It's a learned skill, and definitely not the sort of thing I'd recommend for small children, but the facts are the facts: Once I was cold and then I was not, and now I'm fairly certain that I have discovered something that I'll want to do for the rest of my life.

I haven't brought up my warm underwear with the neighbor for the same reason I haven't mentioned my early-morning musing (especially the stuff about monks and nuns, and death, and that sort of hullabaloo). People don't want to hear about your warm underwear and what puts a smile on your face when they're in the middle of chipping the ice off their windshield or digging a drainage ditch across their front lawn to keep their basement from flooding. Winter is hard on all of us.

I live in a tiny house. I don't mean a small house, the kind with one bedroom, one bathroom, a kitchen, and a nook for watching television, I mean a house the size of an area rug that's easy enough to attach to my truck and drive down the freeway. It looks like a mobile gingerbread house, or a cuckoo clock on wheels. I don't mind the comparisons; I like gingerbread.

The main floor of my house is eighty-four square feet. The sleeping loft that extends over the front porch adds more room. It hangs over the kitchen, bathroom, and closet, and stops about halfway into the center of the house, leaving the living room (what I call the "great room") open to the pointy-roofed ceiling.

Every night, I carry RooDee up the seven-foot ladder to the sleeping loft. We've perfected the process: She takes the form of a fifty-pound soup cauldron, and I pretend it is a piece of cake. There's no drama or exaggerated grunting. No veins bulged, butt cheeks clenched, or near-fatal falls; we operate on autopilot. I lift with my knees, my dog acts like a lead ingot, and together we arrive happy.

My bed consumes most of the loft platform, stretching nearly eave to eave, and from there the roof pitches up to a point four feet above the center of the mattress. That's the line I take: knee-walking down the middle of the bed, taking care not to smash my head into the ceiling. I worm my way into my sleeping bag, under several layers of quilts, and curl into a fetal position with my hands tucked into my armpits. RooDee then rolls into the cave at the back of my knees and we sleep.

I sleep with the blankets over my head, barely moving, directing every ounce of body heat inward until, eventually, I turn into a happy little bun in the oven. I might wake up when the rain starts or stops, when it shifts direction or rolls alongside the house like a tumbleweed, and if I'm lucky I'll catch a break in the rain long enough to see that the moonlight is poking through a giant sphincter of black clouds, like something you'd see in a colonoscopy brochure. Nature has such an odd sense of humor.

I have to admit that, up until now, given the fact that this is my life and my day-to-day routine, my little winter ritual has seemed fairly normal. But just now, writing this, telling you about it, I can see how it might seem unattractive and cold, and perhaps a bit odd. But I don't mind; I've gotten used to it, and I like what it connects me to.

I've come to expect that, regardless of my tender feelings, the Arctic wind will still plunge its way past the San Juan Islands, cleverly sidestepping any number of giant shipping vessels, orca pods, and sea life. It will still gather all manner of rain, sleet, smog, and fog that will shower down persistently for months—enough moisture to fill buckets and barrels, and make city parks into lakes; it will march up the alley like a tempest, kicking the lawn chairs and punching at the carport, and then body-slamming my house. But that's what the wind is programmed to do: work through keyholes and whistle in bottle tops, and make me wonder if my tiny house is being pushed slowly across the lawn like it's rolling through a car wash.

I've gotten used to these sorts of winter high jinks, and to be honest, I like them. I like the excitement of the windstorms and the rain pounding down a thousand different ways, inches from my head. It reminds me of weathering storms while backpacking, climbing, or kayaking—huddling in the dead center of my tent as lightning banged down all around, or hiding from the hail in a blown-out school bus, a piece of junk littering the forest service road that paralleled my hiking trail. The winter weather reminds me that some things never change, and I am still the same girl who loved sleeping in her tree house and who preferred staying outside, and who still thinks reading by head-lamp is romantic.

I like trying to decipher nature's antics, like wondering why there are always more geese on one side of their flying V forma-tion, and why the crocuses have bloomed so early this year. I like that if I'm walking home and I notice that everything seems puckered up, furling inward—the moon, the mud in the lawn, the dried-up tomato plants and cornstalks, the raccoons that hide in the plum tree, and the wind circling the lawn chairs— if they all seem condensed, sucked in, and tight-jawed, then that is a clue for me to follow suit and to curl into a tiny ball with my dog curled into an even smaller ball at my knees. And at the end of the day, when it's all said and done, I usually don't mind that I'm sleeping like a stick figure in a cave painting; that I'm tucked in like the cat sleeping under the hood of the neighbor's car, like the gulls circled up in the marina's mainte-nance barn, or like the adventuresome rabble-rouser I was in my twenties.

I should clarify that I do have a heater—a very nice $500 propane heater that I can turn on and off at will. It has a little exhaust stack that vents out the back of the house, and a tiny glass window in the front that lets me admire the flames as they dart about inside a four-inch-square enclosure. I installed the heater on the back wall of the living room so I could admire it while sitting on the couch. I can also see it from the sleeping loft, a couple of feet away, and from the kitchen and the bathroom. I can study the fire while I cook food or pee or dry off my dog by the front door, when I crack open a beer or take my vitamins, clip my nails or read a book. I can see the heater and its tiny fire from every room of my house because, no matter where I go or what I do, I'm still always in the one room. And therein lies the problem.

My house is roughly the size of a tree stump—a big and tall tree stump, like a giant sequoia that you could drive your car through and then drink hot cocoa on the other side like a tourist, but still a stump of a house, which is why I am afraid of fire. Think about it: A small fire erupts in the living room, which is also the kitchen and dining room, which is also the bedroom and bathroom. It has detonated out of the heater due to some small "oops" in the machinery that causes the tiniest flicker of a flame to brush into the smallest *psssst* of a gas leak. Almost instantly, the fire is massive, a monster devouring the rafters and side walls, collapsing the roof, exploding the canned goods, and buckling the floorboards. In a matter of seconds, my dog and I are left with nowhere to run because there is no other room but this single, highly combustible, highly condensed space the size of a Yule log.

Fire was nothing I'd considered while building my house— not while I was reading about wood grain, kiln-dried lumber, or sustainable forest products; and not while I was hefting great lengths of four-hundred-year-old cedar onto and off my car or even while I was pulling wood out of a pile labeled "Firewood." It never entered my mind as I installed the wood cabinets, the oak toilet seat, and the old fir door, or while I picked sawdust out of my hair and lovingly sanded the smoky smell off the cedar floorboards that had survived someone else's house fire.

Fire wasn't on the agenda until a delivery truck pulled up, weeks into the building project, and dropped off a propane heater. The instruction manual congratulated me for picking a unit that was designed with automatic kill switches in the event of a fire. Apparently, it had state-of-the-art technology, expert tooling, and a brilliant fireproof design with backups for the shut-offs and shutdowns for the turn-offs. *Hummm*, I thought as I thumbed through the manual, *sure wouldn't want a fire*. Then I tossed the manual aside and busied myself with the best place to install the metal firebox.

Months later, on the first cold night of the year, I lit the heater and tucked myself into bed. The fireside glow was beautiful, transforming my small house into a ringside seat at the best mini bonfire ever. Dark amber shadows hung in the corners, and warm firelight gamboled eave to eave along the ceiling, stretching fourteen feet from a spot above the back living room wall to the point above my head.

I sat up in bed for an hour, watching the firelight play tag with the shadows, and I felt myself relax like I hadn't in months. I fell asleep remembering the small campfire my friends and I had made in the Canadian Rockies, in a spot beside a river with snow spires circling the horizon just beyond the forest canopy; that time, I woke up with frost on my eyelashes and the zipper of my bivy sack frozen shut. This time, in my little house, I woke up with my feet twisted up in the sheets. I'd dreamed about racing through a deep thicket, trying to outrun a forest fire, darting with one arm held reflexively over my head and my dog held like a hefty money safe in the other, and all the while the underbrush kept grabbing at my feet, tripping me up, slamming me to the ground. I woke up and looked around the house, realizing for the first time that I'd built a dense, bone-dry tinderbox of a house.

I reread the owner's manual and retraced how I'd installed the heater, double-checking that I hadn't placed insulation too close to the hot flue stack, or exterior siding too close to the exhaust cap. I inspected the smoke detector, nearly deafening myself by clicking the tiny test button. I bought a small bottle of specially made "gas leak detection soap" so I could test every fitting, starting with the knob on the gas tank outside the house and ending with the tiny brass nipple at the base of the heater; I checked again, and then a third time. Everything seemed fine, but at night I still dreamed about fire. I carried a hammer up to the loft so I could smash out the skylight window and launch my dog and me out onto the lawn if necessary, and I dragged a fire extinguisher up the ladder and stationed it between me and the heater like a talisman—a warning to the heater to keep its shit together. Then one night, without really thinking about it, I reached over and flipped off the heater on the way up to bed, giving it a little tap and a smile. And that was the beginning of my nightly bundling routine.

Now I run the heater only during the day and late at night when I am awake, and I hardly notice that I'm dressed like an ice fisherman as I lumber off to bed. Instead, I mosey off to the loft in a not-so-sexy pair of wool underwear, curl into a puffy ball along with RooDee, and together we sleep, happily enough.

These days I find that I am happy enough in the same way that I am warm enough—the goal isn't bliss or even comfort in some cases. The goal is to feel alive, even if the primary proof is the chattering of your teeth. There's nothing like ten-degree weather to redouble your appreciation for wool, fleece, and that odd-looking stocking cap that your mother sent last Christmas.

Admitting that I'm "happy enough" makes me wonder if I'm falling short of my potential as a middle-class American; like I should want more out of life than this tiny house and the backyard, and the way it feels to sit on the porch and watch the sun come up. But it works for me, and besides, I'm not sure that I was any happier when I had a bigger, more normal house.

I used to have a three-bedroom bungalow with a nice yard and massive windows that looked out at the gardens in the front yard. It had a furnace that rumbled away in the basement, thumping, bumping, and popping the ductwork, like it was beating back the cold with a tire iron. I felt very safe from the elements.

The heater was a tireless companion, willing to work day and night, whether we were home or not; it puffed away on metered gas, blowing hot air into the bedrooms and the bathroom, the shampoo bottles and the kitchen silverware drawers. It pushed heat into our bodies, letting us walk around in boxer shorts and tank tops in the middle of winter; it prewarmed our shoes, the toilet seat, the coffee cups. It worked constantly without needing anyone's attention and hardly being noticed at all until the gas bill would arrive and we'd all scream "Turn down the thermostat!" and grow very quiet.

The heating bill usually arrived a few days after the electric bill, which came two weeks after the mortgage and insurance were due; then the water, sewer, and trash bill would arrive every three months, and the property taxes would arrive like Satan on a stick once a year. Somewhere in the mix were my monthly credit card bills, tied to all the other necessary household items: a couch, television, window shades, barbecue grill, new hot water tank, bedsheets, telephone, stereo speakers, flower vases, a shower curtain, washing machine, area rugs, garden hoses, lamps, lights, locks, a spade, mattresses, memory foam pillows, wineglasses, a dishwasher, lawn mower, end tables, two cubic yards of garden compost, scrub brushes, butter knives, a refrigerator, wrenches, pry bars, and an assortment of artwork and wall paint to make things look nice. I worked hard back then, strapped to my debt, but I was hardly miserable; I was happy enough "living the dream" as I raced from one place to the next and spent the weekends cleaning the gutters or reading a how-to book on home plumbing repair.

Now that I live in my little house, I work part-time and pay eight dollars a month for utilities. There's no mortgage, no Saturday morning with a vacuum, mop, or dust cloth. I have free time to notice the weather, so if my neighbor asks me how it's going, I can easily explain how "the barometric pressure took a real nosedive at four this morning, causing a lava flow of cooler air to pour into my house through the open windows. It was like waking up in Missoula in September, when you still have your windows open but know things are changing, and quick, toward winter."

All the time I save leaves me free to cavort and volunteer, building other little houses with friends, helping to care for my elderly neighbor, or staring mindlessly at the clouds forming into balloon animals and broccoli spears. The other day I spent a couple of hours packing sauerkraut with my friends, nattering about local politics while we shoved stinky cabbage into little jars. Before that, I collected a load of fruit to be delivered all over town as part of a church fund-raiser, and then I took my dog for a walk down along the old railroad trestle that used to be the shake mill but is now just a massive expanse of busted-up asphalt, blackberry bushes, and Scotch broom. It's actually quite beautiful down there, loaded with herons, otters, salmon, and seals; stunning despite the shopping carts that the kids have drowned in the mud and the yellow warning signs about contaminated shellfish.

It's nice to have time to amble around, or do whatever I want; to drop everything and help the neighbor build a chicken coop, or hop in on a spontaneous game of Pickle-ball in the backyard. A year or so after I moved into my house, I volunteered to show it in a green building fair, an event that included vendors like the ReBuilding Center and Habitat for Humanity, as well as local homeowners who had installed solar electric systems, recycled fir floors, and energy-efficient windows in their houses. While I didn't have fancy systems in my house, I still figured it'd be helpful if people saw how beautiful salvaged cedar siding can be, and how wonderful a door pulled out of a dumpster (like mine) could be.

At the fair, I met a teacher who thought it'd be nice to show her students my house, and that's how a few months later I found myself hosting sixty-four fourth-graders in my yard. They were studying global climate change and asked some very important questions like where do I poop, where's the bathtub, and why not build a giant slingshot to shoot my dog into the loft instead of having to carry her? They wanted to know if I was happy living without a television, without running water, and without space for a "husband" (whoever he was). I offered a quick "Heck yeah!" and then suggested that we all try to fit into the house at one time; it would be the "New International, Intergalactic, Ripley's Believe It or Not, Hotshot, Full-of-Snot Record!" I screamed. All sixty-four of them raced into the house, stood on the toilet, piled onto the kitchen counter, smashed into the loft, and squeezed into the living room like a jar of human pickles. Everyone was giggling and I was thinking this was a great teaching moment, where they'd finally come to see that even something teeny-tiny can be big *enough*, and that's when tragedy struck: Someone "cut the cheese," as my brothers would say, and the entire class emptied out of the house in seconds like clowns pouring out of a circus car. We all collapsed on the lawn, fake-coughing and laughing hysterically, and intensely proud of the new record we'd set.

I probably overemphasized how glorious everything is, using the word *awesome* too many times. I positively gushed about how *awesome* it was to live debt free, not really considering whether any of those kids fully understood how crushing it is to juggle bills, delicately staggering the payments throughout the month and shuffling money from one credit card to another. And they probably thought I was full of shit when I said it was *awesome* to live without a television and refrigerator, "free from that infernal, constant humming and drumming so now I can hear the tree frogs at night . . . blah blah blah."

If I had been perfectly honest, I would have admitted that I'm happy only 85 percent of the time, roughly three hundred days out of the year. The other days, I wish I had running water or that the house was warmer; or I might want a seventy-two-inch plasma screen television and enough space to invite all my friends over to watch the Oscars. I might want a flushing toilet and an endless supply of cheap beer, and a cutie-pie to play naked Scrabble with me in the living room. I might want more privacy and solitude, and for the city to get new garbage trucks so on Friday mornings I wouldn't have to listen to all that hydraulic whining with heavy lifting and slamming back down. I might *want* a lot of things . . . but that doesn't mean I *need* them.

Here's the raw truth: 15 percent of the time, you might find me grousing while slopping my water back to the house, or pouting about how I don't like going to the laundromat to watch my underwear occasionally float by in the viewing window of the nearby clothes dryer. My complaining might result in my stomping off to bed, where I'll check out of my life and watch three or four episodes of *Battlestar Galactica* on my laptop computer screen. In the morning, I'll wake up late for work, cuss, and quickly yank rain pants over my pajamas so I can rush off to the office, where I'll spend most of the day trying not to make loud plastic-pant crinkling and swooshing noises, and hoping that everyone believes I've just arrived from doing something important outside.

Those are the days that most remind me of my old life in my big house where I'd charge around and act like the world owes me more; or where I'd rush through the days and watch television at night, and at the end of the week I couldn't remember if I'd actually called my mother or simply wished that I had.

Now, more often than not, instead of feeling pissed at the rain for turning my bones into soggy oatmeal, I'll walk over to my friends' house and they'll make me laugh and feed me warm soup; or, in the case of a particularly hateful moment with my composting toilet, I'll remember watching the little kids in Guatemala roll up their pants cuffs and walk across the muddy mess that was overflowing from the school's bathroom, and I'll realize I have nothing to complain about. I'll remember like an apple to the head that I'm lucky to have what I have and that I'm not entitled to any more than those kids, or their fathers, whom we'd see walking along the roads at dawn, carrying their machetes out into the fields for the day.

"My house is warm enough" is what I might eventually realize as I fall asleep mummified in my sleeping bag, and later I'll wake up to see that the clouds are sprinting across the moon like a movie where the director wants you to think time is passing very quickly. Nature can be kind like that.

I chose the 85 percent success rate, starting with the crazy decision to build the house myself, one stick of wood at a time; then the decision to build the house on wheels so I could come and go as I please. I chose this path because the idea of building a house sounded like the old, fun me—the woman who thought it was a total jazz-up to hang by her thumbs fifty feet in the air, scaling some rocky crag to get a better view of the valley below. I chose this because I thought I could be happy living in a one-room house without running water or a refrigerator, and I imagined I'd learn something about myself by stripping myself down to the basics—by living with two dinner plates, three spoons, two pairs of pants, a dress, and my wool skivvies. And I figured I could be happy, at least for a while, living in the shadow of my friends Hugh and Annie's house, in their old garden plot just off the alley.

I thought I'd find something in all of this, and I got more than I bargained for. I discovered a new way of looking at the sky, the winter rain, the neighbors, and myself; and a different way of spending my time. Most important, I stumbled into a new sort of "happiness," one that didn't hinge on always getting what I want, but rather, on wanting what I have. It's the kind of happiness that isn't tied so tightly to being comfortable (or having money and property), but instead is linked to a deeper sense of satisfaction—to a sense of humility and gratitude, and a better understanding of who I am in my heart.

I know this sounds cheesy, and in fact, it sounds fairly similar to the gobbledygook that friends have thrown at me just after having their first baby. But the facts are the facts: I found

a certain bigness in my little house—a sense of largeness, freedom, and happiness that comes when you see there's no place
else you'd rather be.

I found myself at Home, and that is (as I hope to tell the
next set of fourth-graders) *awesome*!

Southeast State Park

(PORTLAND, OREGON, APRIL 2003)

I was standing in the bathroom of my former house, nervously chewing the inside of my cheek, holding a how-to book in one hand and a screwdriver in the other. This was the fortieth time I'd tried to figure out why the bathroom fuse kept tripping when someone ran the vacuum upstairs or when we flipped on the garbage disposal in the kitchen. It made no sense; the electric lines that ran upstairs and to the kitchen were on different circuits, and according to my book, everything should work.

I clicked the light switch, and as expected, nothing happened. I set the book aside and climbed halfway up the ladder that I had positioned under the light globe. I unscrewed the fixture to unhinge it from the ceiling and pulled on it to dislodge the wires. I'd seen this at a friend's house, and the light fixture was supposed to dangle six or eight inches below the ceiling, hanging off the wires like a dinner plate suspended by metal twisty-ties; but my dinner plate only moved a little, allowing me just enough space to jam in the screwdriver and stir it around like a cocktail twirler, which turned out to be a bad idea. There was a pistol pop and a flash of light, and I fell backward off the ladder with a loud "Aaaak!" I lay there for a while, catching my breath and reflecting on my situation.

It was my own fault, and maybe that's why I found this particular home improvement project so painful. I had rewired the bathroom years ago, just a few weeks after my friends and I had sledgehammered out the old wall plaster and dragged the ancient toilet out the front door, scrunching up our faces and nearly puking along the way. We'd pried up the curling linoleum and crowbarred the moldy subfloor until we could see, between the floor joists, the basement concrete resting eight feet below. I had hired a friend to retile the shower, agreeing to pay her about half the going rate but still twice what I had in my checking account; then, before she got started, I hired a plumber to install a new faucet. It didn't seem like much work: running a short piece of copper pipe from the basement up through the wall, then stubbing it out to receive the new fixtures. I thought it would take an hour or so—easy-peasy—and a half hour after he arrived, he handed me a bill for three hundred bucks. I almost cried, and then I got mad. He wasn't a bad guy, of course. The problem was that I was a new homeowner, suffering from sticker shock and exhausted by the buckets of money I had been handing off to the bank, the realtor, the title company, the IRS, and the City of Portland. Even the lock-smith, an older gentleman who reminded me of my grandpa, had gotten a slice of my dwindling pie. I shadowed him as he worked, partially because I was truly fascinated but also be-cause I wanted him to like me, to take pity on me and cut me a deal, but all he did was wink and say, "You're safe now," as he handed me a set of keys and a bill for a hundred fifty dollars.

A few days later, as I was standing in line at the hardware store, I picked up a how-to book that illustrated the best way to fix a drippy faucet, tuck-point a chimney, sheetrock your den, build a deck, replace window glass, install insulation, and re-pair a door latch. It was amazing, like the book was made for me and my old house and my puny bank account. *If I'd had this earlier, I probably could have soldered those pipes myself,* I thought, *and I can certainly rewire the bathroom!*

This is what happens to people who grow up believing that books perform like tiny life rafts, saving students from having to take the GRE blind, rescuing cooks from bland, overcooked dumplings, and keeping homeowners afloat by reassuring them that they can do it all on their own.

I suddenly grew cocky as I stood there with that book, pos-itive that I could figure out the electrical work, which should have been a piece of cake (based on the fact that there were only three pages dedicated to this extremely simple activity).

After a few weeks and several long, confused conversations

with the men at the hardware store, I was able to connect new lights, a fan, and outlets to the fuse box in the basement. I closed my eyes the first time I turned on the system, clicking the breaker in the fuse box, worried that a giant spark would lunge out at my head, but nothing bad happened. The thing worked; the lights came on and the blow-dryer clicked on, and I got a little dizzy with the success of it all. "Oh my God." I laughed at my little electricity pun. *I* rewired the bathroom; *I* achieved 100 percent success! I did a little victory lap around the living room with my hands over my head like I'd just kicked a winning field goal.

The electrical system worked perfectly for nearly a year, until, by chance, I turned on a vacuum cleaner upstairs while Holly, my housemate, was blow-drying her hair in the bathroom. There was a small *pffft* at the wall outlets, and we both lost use of our appliances.

At first, I tried hard to solve the problem, working from memory to draw a picture of the wires and splices that were now hidden in the walls. I consulted with an electrician friend, and stood with him in the basement, staring up at the squirrel nest of pipes and wires that ran below the kitchen, bathroom, dining room, and living room. The previous owner had done most of the work himself, leaving my friend shaking his head and sighing, "This is sadistic." More time went by, and then, as the edges of my interest got picked apart by other home repair projects, I let go of the need for perfection and resigned myself to occasionally stomping down to the breaker box to flip the blown bathroom fuse.

No one had explained the challenges of home ownership when I went to the bank for a home loan. I was thirty-four, and perhaps the unspoken assumption was that I was old enough to understand that this was a complicated investment. The bank loan would have to cover more than just the house; I'd also need cash for a ladder and several how-to books, and an assortment of other necessary objects to make things right. I would need to buy paint and devote several hours to picking just the right color—not green or orange, but Winter Sage and Tuscany Sunset.

My loan officer didn't bring up the other costs; there was no mention of his first house, and how he spent a small fortune on coffee because he stayed up late worrying about the way his roof leaked—a leak that persisted even though he'd dared himself to shimmy up onto the roof in the middle of a rain storm, hanging onto the roof shingles like a cat on a screen door, so he could caulk the roof vent. It was a leak that he had finally "fixed" by shoving a plastic pan (an old kitty litter tray) in just the right spot, so all night long he could listen to the rain *plink-plink-plink* in the pan. "And that noise was worse than the leak itself!"

He didn't say that at the time, though he would tell me all

this later. Instead, he encouraged me to fill out some paperwork for a loan, and "If you qualify," the loan officer said, "we'll help you get into the best possible house."

The "best possible" sounded dreamy. Even though I didn't recognize it, I was drawn to living just like my parents, in a reasonable house, with a beautiful family, where we'd have a Christmas tree in the living room, and every Sunday we'd have pot roast. On some level, in some unspoken, undefined way, I imagined that, by buying a house, I would finally arrive into my adulthood; my parents would begin calling me for advice, and my inclination for doing stunts that began with the words "Hey, watch this" would fade. I'd settle down and fall in love responsibly, instead of sacking impish rock climbers who lived on their boats or in their parents' basement, or in their old pot-soaked Volkswagen van tricked out for camping. Home ownership would bring me credibility and respect, and approving nods from all manner of respectable, responsible adults.

I qualified for a $200,000 loan that I could pay back over thirty years. I remember sitting at the bank, sweating in my raincoat and sipping complimentary coffee out of a styrofoam cup, listening to the banker explain the terms of my loan. None of the numbers made sense—how could someone like me, a state worker making less than a schoolteacher, qualify for a nearly quarter-million-dollar loan? How could I plan for a thirty-year payback when I was still loath to commit to a weekend backpacking trip? Sitting there, I supposed I was simply lucky; my ship had arrived.

Shortly after that, I started driving around with a real estate agent, a lanky six-foot-tall woman who wore long gauzy scarves and a leather trench coat. Her excessive bigness made me feel safe, which was important given the fact that the house-buying process had reduced me to a twelve-year-old. She reassured me that home ownership was a snap, talking about the amazing "sense of home" (something akin to cinnamon buns and warm slippers) that arises through owning a house. She never mentioned that, the day before, she'd walked into a house that had been sealed up and neglected for nearly a year, and she'd almost turned and run away, then grabbed her scarf and wadded it over her mouth and nose, hiding from the overwhelming smell of mold and mildew, and the way the ceilings, walls, curtains, drapes, couch, and every other nappy surface in the structure was covered with a gray-black fuzz. "It was like an episode of *The X-Files*," she'd told me months later, when I asked what was the creepiest house she'd ever been in.

Instead, she focused on the positive, and we gleefully began looking at the "best possible" houses, which I imagined would be something cute with a nice yard, in a good neighborhood where I could walk to the bus and ride my bike to my friends' houses. Within an hour of driving around, I realized she was showing me only dumpy houses that were occupied by sad peo-

ple who seemed resigned to their lives with moldy bathrooms,
peeling paint, and a view of a flashing "Bare Naked" strip club
sign. At first, I wondered if my agent had bad taste, or maybe
she thought that I had bad taste—that I was attracted to houses
that looked hungover, or that I would somehow find comfort in
living next to the local bottle factory. After the fifth fixer-
upper—a vacant house with porn videos in the upstairs
bathroom—it dawned on me that this was what my life savings
and thirty years of debt would get me: a lumpy, scabby house
that needed a lot of love and elbow grease; that's what $200,000
and thirty years of monthly payments could buy in Portland,
Oregon.

A few weeks later, in the winter of 1997, I bought what the
bank believed was the best possible house: a three-bedroom
bungalow with a detached garage, wood floors, gas heat, and a
fireplace. It was in an up-and-coming neighborhood, within
walking distance of the grocery store, the bus, my friends, the
bank, pubs, and restaurants. On paper, it was perfect; in real
life, it was a "piece of crap," as I had scribbled in my notebook
when the realtor and I had visited.

My new house was an old house, built in 1927, when it was
customary to set rings into the concrete sidewalk out front so
your friends could tether their horse when they came to visit. It
was an old house that seemed to have good bones, that may
even have been a looker in its day but now reminded me of a
boozy, broken-down prizefighter with two foggy windows on

either side of the droopy bump-out porch, like it was squinting at the street, growling, "I could have been a contender" every time someone walked by.

It wasn't quite what I had envisioned. The front living room, an expansive room that needed a lot of repair, became the woodshop. For nearly a year, when I'd walk through the front door, I'd confront an assortment of paint cans, tools, tile supplies, and a couple of eighteen-foot wood-skinned kayaks set up on sawhorses. For months, when I needed a break from working on the house, I worked on my kayak.

I never would have guessed that my new improved life and the "best possible" house would include an occasional rat sighting (something that would vex me for at least two years) or a refrigerator that you had to aggressively hug and then knee to get the door closed, but it wasn't so bad. And more important: It was all mine!

I was the boss, and by setting the rent low, I was able to recruit friends and friends of friends to move in. Together we lived happily enough, with lumpy futon mattresses and three-legged chairs, and lamps and cups and dinner plates dragged home from garage sales or "Free" boxes. We once pushed a couch six blocks and through heavy traffic by balancing it on a skateboard, only to discover as we dragged it up the front stairs that it was infested with fleas and that a rat had made a nest in the bottom springs. We quickly reloaded it onto the skateboard and backtracked, screaming and laughing and scratching our scalps. Living on a budget may have been more fun than any of us cared to admit.

Over the next six years, I had eight different housemates—nine if I count Jenna, who moved in temporarily, sleeping in a small, unheated room off the kitchen that we called the "recycling porch." It was a sweet room, not much bigger than a single bed, but surrounded by south-facing windows that created one of the more spacious, sunny spots in the house. Jenna moved in for a few weeks, but stayed for six months, until it got too cold on the porch, and she found a job and an apartment across town.

Before Jenna left, she turned her room into what would become one of my favorite spots in the house, repainting it a warm red-orange color and building bookshelves above the door, the window, and the coat hooks she'd screwed into the plaster. She made a comfortable enough bed out of plywood and a lawn chair cushion, and then permanently inscribed poems and pinned tiny bits of artwork on the window jambs. The space reminded me of the small hay-bale clubhouses and scrap-wood tree forts that my brothers and I had made as kids—high-up spaces where you could see things differently, where you could get your bearings and decide whether the argument you'd just had was fixable.

We eventually returned Jenna's room to the recycling bins, but I'd still sometimes find myself standing there, catching my breath and reading the stuff that Jenna had scribbled on the walls and painted into the woodwork, imagining how simple things would be if the only space I had to vacuum was this tiny button of a room.

My weekend trips to the hardware store had slowly taken the place of my weekends in the mountains, and after a while I couldn't remember the last time I'd touched my climbing gear except perhaps to dig for some art supplies I'd packed away in the boxes below it. I convinced myself that my house projects weren't that different from climbing: They almost always involved some moment of fear—that I'd shoot myself off the ladder, nail my foot to the floor, or run a saw through the plumbing—and that moment was almost always followed by immediate relief. In either case (fear or relief) I felt like a champion because I was figuring shit out. I was a doer and a getter-doner, and it was okay to be identified by the neighbors as the little lady who had a dump truck of manure delivered, a load that made the entire neighborhood smell like a dairy barn for weeks.

I figured these house projects were making me smart, even if I didn't always know what I was doing. I remember calling an equipment rental place one Valentine's Day weekend, telling them I needed to rent a fourteen-inch "vibrator," assuming this was the common word for the large vibrating pad sander I needed to refinish my wood floors. The guy laughed into the phone: "Ha, you and every other woman in Portland!" I was so caught up in the project, in getting the equipment and cracking a whip, that it took me a minute to get his joke.

Another day, I wanted to trim some branches off the big fir tree in the front yard; I didn't want it to take long, just a quick up and down, so I left the ladder in the garage and scrambled up the fir with a tree saw in my mouth. New neighbors were moving in next door, ushering boxes up their front stairs, when I dropped out of the tree near their porch to say hello and welcome them to the neighborhood. They gave me very uneasy looks as I stood there, and then suddenly seemed to amp up their need to "get moving." A few minutes later, I went into my house to pee, and as I washed my hands I noticed in the bathroom mirror that I was sporting half of a Fu Manchu mustache—long, bushy hair that started just below my left nostril and ended near my chin. My best guess was that I'd inadvertently wiped tree sap on my face and then nuzzled my dog, thus creating a curious wad of facial hair for the new neighbors to ponder. I spent the next month cleverly trying to catch them as they left their house, hoping to offer a casual "Hello" and show off my hair-free face to restart our first meeting.

The hard work (and possible social isolation) paid off, and over time, the house became home. The front living room was repaired, the woodshop was moved to the garage, and our lumpy couch was replaced with a nicer one—one that I bought from the want ads and that didn't come with fleas and rats. The kitchen floor was replaced and new appliances were installed, and the house's shabby exterior was rehabilitated, resheathed, and painted to look handsome and capable again.

In early summer one year, I cut open the back wall and installed two large glass doors so you could wander from the kitchen through the dining room into the backyard. Then I rehabbed the backyard into a little sanctuary, building a brick fire pit in the center of the lawn, not far from the deck that I salvaged from a friend's house, one ten-foot chunk at a time, maxing out the load capacity of my car along with my luck.

On summer nights, my friends and I would gather at "Southeast State Park" (their nickname for my yard), and we'd throw open the glass doors so that whatever was happening in the kitchen could drain onto the deck and then spill toward the fire ring, where we'd set up our lawn chairs. That feeling of air and people floating unobstructed from one room to the next, from inside to out, was one of the best things about my house. Even in the winter, the big glass doors and windows supported that sense of openness.

///////////////////////

I loved my house, but when I look back at it realistically, I was able to enjoy it only a small part of the time. Most of my time at home was focused on mowing the grass, repairing the hot water heater, cleaning the gutters, and trying to keep the garage from listing farther into the neighbor's yard—that's how I spent most of my waking hours at home. And more and more, the chance to enjoy my house was even more cramped because of my long-distance commute, racing back and forth for work and up to Olympia, a hundred miles away, which is why I'd chosen this particular moment to try (once again) to repair the bathroom fuse. Once again, the attempt left me slumped on the floor at the base of a ladder, yelling, "Akkkk," but at least I was trying. And I could always clomp down the stairs to flip the breaker like always, like this is what homeowners do, and what I'd likely have to do again next month or some other day when I least expected it.

The Drive

(PORTLAND, OREGON, OCTOBER 2003)

Last night, as I was driving home from work in a downpour, I slammed on my brakes after spotting three kittens about to saunter across the highway. I pulled over to the shoulder, then backed up, watching for them in the glow of the taillights. I wasn't sure what I would do if I caught up with my little fuzz balls but was certain that something needed to be done. I hate seeing roadkill, and dead kittens would just crush me inside.

I got back to what I thought must be the spot and looked around, scanning the area through the rain and flipping the windshield wipers, craning my neck over the steering wheel as I flipped on the high beams and then the low, and then I spun around in my seat to squint through the dim light behind the car. "Crap," I muttered, unclicking the seat belt and angrily pulling my hood over my head, then pausing to look in the rearview mirror for traffic.

People get killed on the highway. Years ago, my sister was nearly hit when she got a flat tire along the interstate. She had done everything right, crawling out the passenger-side door to avoid the highway traffic—a near act of God because she was nine and a half months pregnant and the size of a small army. She got to the trunk to pull out the spare and that's when a semi came by and the wind shear nearly knocked her in a ditch. A passing motorist saw it—saw my sister in her tan wool coat that wouldn't button over her belly anymore—so he stopped and changed the tire as my sister sat in the car, biting her lip, fearful that this stranger would help her and then pop her in the head with the tire iron. We were taught not to offer or invite aid because, like it or not, helping is a messy, confused proposition; sometimes you get it right and sometimes you get it wrong, and sometimes you have no choice but to trust that the man holding your tire iron, cussing at your old lug nuts, is a deeply kind human after all.

I threw open the car door and stepped into the rain, quickly skirting around the car to the far side of the highway shoulder. "Here, kitty-kitty-kitty," I shouted in a singsong that I hoped could be heard over the rain. I continued walking inside the beam of my headlights, scanning the ditch as I walked, and seeing something that for a moment made my heart skip: a dead kitty that turned out to be a shoe. Ready to give up, I turned to walk back, and a movement by my car caught my eye; a hairy ball crept out from under the car. I got closer, shading my eyes from the headlights and wondering what the hell I'd do with the cat once I caught her, and a moment later, as I bent down to pick her up, I realized I was staring at a baby raccoon barely the size of a beer mug. "Shit!" I whispered as a semitruck plowed by, causing me to do a sidestep and tumbling the kit.

"Hi, little fella," I said, squatting down on my haunches and wringing my hands together like I was holding a bug, afraid to reach out for the animal. In my mind, although raccoons are cute and I love how they can walk around holding an ear of corn in their mitts just like small children at a picnic, they inhabit the general category of fearful creatures called "varmints." Like rats, they carry diseases, have teeth, and show up when least expected, like when you're moving a stack of old flower pots in your garage; they are vicious when cornered and run in packs like street thugs.

"Where's your mama?"

The baby suddenly veered left toward the ditch and sped up, like it was drawn by some imperceptible voice shouting, "NO-O-O-O! Do not walk toward the human!" I stood up and examined the ditch near my car, where I could finally see three sets of eyes looking back at me: two smaller sets (kits) and a larger, meaner set (their mother), which spun me on my heels and sent me racing to the car. I jumped in, yelped, and slammed the door behind me.

That was weird, I thought as I clutched the steering wheel, sighing in relief. Then another monstrous truck drove by, shaking my car and causing me to panic. My neck muscles were tighter than piano strings and I had a headache. I just wanted to be home; to walk into the living room and see my housemates up late and studying by the fireplace, to chitchat for a few minutes before wandering off.

I sighed and started the car. "Good luck, my friends," whispering to the mother as I pulled forward along the shoulder. "Be safe."

I was on the road too much lately. I knew it, and I was glad it would soon change.

///////////////////

At about the same time I purchased my new old house, I took a job as a State Hazardous Waste Inspector, which entailed popping in on various businesses to see how they were managing their chemicals. I'd check to see that they were abiding by the law, that acid wasn't dribbling into the workers' boots or out the back door, and that local farm boys out hunting weren't going to fall in a hole filled with a thousand gallons of waste, something dumped and forgotten and so hot it would incinerate their legs within seconds. It was a perfect job for a person like me—someone curious and fidgety (according to some), and averse to sitting at a desk for too long—and it gave me a chance to see how things were made: imitation crab legs, bullets, paper plates, car batteries, applesauce, tar paper, wool blankets, bicycles, ballistic missiles, shiny water nozzles, and little horseshoe-shaped grills destined for use at a taco shell factory. Like a kid touring the local cookie factory, I looked forward to finding out what ingredients went into the production of a solar panel, a wine bottle, sticky tape, and biodegradable soap. The only real downside was that people often didn't like to see me. A visit from my cronies and me was akin to getting frisked by a cop or audited by the IRS. It was like having your teeth cleaned, and like any good dentist who learned to stand beyond the kicking radius of his patient, I learned to duck and cover, and to steel myself against the wave of ill will that sometimes surged toward me when I walked in the door.

I took classes and workshops, and studied various workbooks and manuals. I read and reread the law, highlighted various sections of the rulebook, and listened hard to what my mentors were saying. I even attended a class at the Federal Law Enforcement Training Center in Georgia, where I thought I'd learn to shoot a gun but instead simply learned that, at lunch, it was better not to picnic in the grassy area near the obstacle course because nearly every day a SWAT team would suddenly materialize out of the kudzu to charge across the field in their black commando outfits and practice busting down a door with a battering ram.

My class wasn't as action-packed; we marched around in the woods, pretending to collect evidence off a truck that supposedly had flipped over and dumped drums full of chromic acid across the road. The truck and drums were there, tucked in the woods with the humidity, no-see-ums, and fire ants; the only part that was missing was the toxic waste—that part we had to imagine.

The main lesson I learned from this activity was that my job was a cakewalk compared with those of my classmates— Virginia State Troopers, New York City Police, Texas Rangers, and bomb squad guys. We stayed up late one night, lounging around on pool chairs under a flashing neon hotel sign, talking loud enough to be heard over the nearby highway noise and the grind of a nearby ice machine. We horsed around, flipping bottle caps over the pool, then tossing a pizza box like a Frisbee until it sailed over the fence into the highway chaff. At one point, as we were shooting the shit, I asked a general question like: "Have you ever been so afraid or freaked out that you peed your pants?" We were well into our beers and I figured this group of smart-asses would make some wisecrack like: "You mean besides the moment I saw your scrawny ass walk in the room?" But instead, they got quiet and reached into the cooler for another beer.

A guy from New York told a story about responding to a call about "shots fired" in an affluent neighborhood. He arrived at the address and ran up to the front porch, when all of a sudden the front door flew open and he found himself eye to eye with the gunman: an eight-year-old boy who turned and bolted up a flight of stairs, firing a shot over his shoulder as he ran. "He looked at me like my own boy does, like when I've caught him playing on his computer after I've told him to go to bed," the cop said as he stared into the can he was rolling between his palms. He made fun of himself, cackling that he had gotten so knock-kneed, he had to hide in the bushes for twenty minutes, trying to get his shit together so he could walk back to his patrol car to radio for help.

One of the guys from Colorado gave a single nod, and in a tone barely audible over the ice maker, said, "Ya, I know that feeling." He didn't need to say more; we knew he was one of the first people to enter Columbine High School after a couple of students had opened fire, killing thirteen people and injuring dozens more. This guy, now sitting on a deck chair beside me, had done his job and waddled into the school, wearing a blast suit: puffy padding, a twenty-pound helmet, and other protective gear appropriate for finding and defusing bombs. We all knew what he must have seen—the media broadcasts lingered for weeks after the event—but no amount of imagination (of hearing accounts and reading reports, or seeing the kind of special effects horror that finds its way to television and movies) could capture what he must have experienced walking into Columbine, or how the images of backpacks, upended tables, chairs, books, and blood splatter may have lodged themselves deep inside his understanding of the world. It took hours to clear the building of nearly a hundred bombs—hours that must have felt like years to everyone involved, especially, maybe, the bomb squad.

No one said anything for a minute, and I felt embarrassed, complete with burning cheeks and red ears, for asking the question in such a flippant way. Sitting there, I realized I was out of my depth with these guys. I was just a state worker with nothing to talk about except maybe the day the copy machine jammed and I panicked because I had a huge meeting that required a printed agenda. More than that, I recognized that I was small and soft; I wanted to believe in people—that they were kind and good, and given the chance, everything would turn out okay—but bad things *do* happen, and sometimes the best you can do is swim through them, focus, and years later say, "Ya, I know that feeling," when some smart ass asks whether you've ever been so scared you wanted to pee your pants.

In my first year on the job, the worst thing I ever saw was a poisoned fishpond. It was a man-made pond, smaller than a 7-Eleven parking lot, and stocked with big goldfish and koi— ornamental, expendable fish that lured hungry herons, falcons, raccoons, and other varmints from the river nearby. A drum of paint thinner had been dumped into the pond through a storm-water drain, and I ended up standing on the pond bank, arguing with a man nearly a foot and a half taller than me—a massive mountain of a man with hair bulging out from around the shoulder straps of his T-shirt—arguing that he had broken the law. He yelled that it didn't matter; it was his pond, his fish, his property, and the state could shove off. After a few minutes, he stormed off to call his lawyer, and I stood there watching as a thousand tiny fish bobbed up to the pond surface, seeming to paw at the air with their mouths gaping and their fins slowly circling, and then one by one they listed sideways and died with their eyes wide open, staring at me like I had failed them.

I nearly cried while standing by the pond, and pouted for hours afterward, chiding myself that I should have thrown absorbent pads into the water instead of arguing. Or maybe, instead of feeling so righteous and indignant, I could have grabbed a rake and pulled some of the living fish into a pail. I swore to myself that's what I'd do if I ever came across a dying pond again.

Over time, I realized I wasn't necessarily seeing people or things at their best or worst; instead, I was simply seeing things as they were.

There didn't seem to be a moral high road to take in most situations, and "What's the right thing to do?" wasn't an easy question, even though I assumed the answers would get easier once I came to understand how to best wield the skinny rulebook that I packed in my gear bag. My field notes became dotted with little sidebar observations that couldn't be readily explained: "Man used severed horse leg as stopper in floor drain" at a rendering plant, and "Canada geese landed on corrosive settling pond. Did not melt; seems they should have."

My job exposed me to the real world, and the more I saw (like the fact that nature was all up inside what I once believed was simply industrial, and how people are willing to crawl on their elbows for a paycheck), the more I realized how limited my field of vision was. I was protected and privileged, and to be honest, I didn't really want to know what it took to make the copper cookware that I ogled at the store—cookware that I wanted to dangle from hooks near the stovetop, fleshing out my kitchen and making it appear that I was capable and clever, and ready to create a feast at a moment's notice. I have never cooked like that and would probably just use one of those copper-bottomed pots to make popcorn.

Over time, I discovered that learning new things doesn't always liberate you. Instead, it makes you wonder if your pants are on backward or if the trees are holding the sky up—it makes you question all of your assumptions and conventions. Some nights when I got home from work, I'd find myself mowing the grass, cleaning the gutters, or retesting the bathroom's electrical system (once again pulling out the short ladder and grabbing a screwdriver for support) while I rattled my head as if a bee had flown in my ear, trying to make sense out of what I'd just witnessed (a taxidermist boiling skulls in a common kitchen pot; a hatch of frogs living on the walls surrounding acid baths). On those days, I imagined that a better world would be less complicated, less involved, and with less need to mass-produce doorknobs and lock sets, electric outlets, power cords, frozen chicken wings, packages of steak, rubber bands, and a million little foam earbuds that slip over the broadcasting end of an iPod. I'd stand staring at Jenna's room, the recycling porch, and imagine what my life would be like if I could squeeze all my worldly possessions into a space like that.

///////////////////////

My normal commute into work was about fifteen or twenty minutes—as long as it took to snake through the never-ending construction in my "up-and-coming" neighborhood, past the condos being built near the railroad tracks, the hardware store, corner grocery store, music shop, pub, and appliance repair place; past the place that used to make bowling trophies but is now a swank restaurant, and the old Ford factory, where back in the day they'd assemble cars on the third floor, then use an elevator to lower them down to the first floor so they could be rolled onto train cars for distribution. I drove less than

five miles through my neighborhood, where everything seemed
to be turning into the "perfect place"—a perfect coffee shop,
vintage clothing boutique, restaurant, or pub, which sold the
same beer as the old place but with higher prices; and then I'd
hop on the interstate.

Every morning, there was a moment of decision making, a
nanosecond where I'd imagine heading south into the sunshine,
toward San Francisco, then Los Angeles, and then Mexico; or
maybe I'd detour out of L.A. into Joshua Tree National Park, to
climb the slabs and sit in the open air for a while. Instead, I'd
go north to my office, ten minutes away, just over the Columbia
River, except that, for the past few months, on Mondays, I had
to continue north another hundred miles to Olympia. There,
I'd sit through meetings, stare into a computer screen, and
otherwise spend a few days trapped in a gargantuan building
that had to pump "white noise" into the workspaces (a constant
statticky sound) to keep workers from going mad with the
overwhelming clitter-clatter of a hundred computer keyboards,
telephone conversations, watercooler gaffes, and slowly ticking
wall clocks. It was a temporary situation, "a moment of transi-
tion," my boss had said, where for six months I would be the
acting unit supervisor and all of my coworkers would do the
best they could to put up with the fact that I had no idea how to
supervise.

There was too much paperwork and not enough fieldwork,
and I hated being the person that people would call when they

were sick. I didn't like having to hear about their personal problems—the baby puking; kids with measles, flu, lice, or diarrhea; there was colitis, impacted molars, and the need to stay home and wait for a new hot water heater to be delivered. There seemed to be a steady stream of very specific problems, and I was a lousy supervisor because even while I was saying something like "Oh my, that's rough," I didn't really want to hear about how the toilet had overflowed and then the car wouldn't start. I didn't want to know about so-and-so's aunt dying and how everyone was getting together at her house.

It wasn't that I didn't care; it was just so fatiguing to hear how horrible everyone's life was, because that's all you hear when people call in sick. No one calls in sick because they're in love or because they can't fathom spending another minute away from their toddler. I was no different; every Sunday night, rain or shine, in love or not, I packed a small bag, loaded my dog and me into the car, and drove north to Olympia.

Fortunately, there was an end to the madness and a new supervisor was in the works. I just needed to hang in there for another month, and enjoy the fact that the drive up to Olympia brought me closer to my friends a few days a week.

I had lived in Olympia for six years before moving down to Portland, so it was nice to hang out with Candyce and Paula, whose living room floor ended up being my crash pad for a couple nights each week. We had kept in touch after I moved, but there's something that shifts when you have time to stumble into one another on the way to the coffeepot early in the morning.

Along the same line, it was good to see Hugh and Annie more often, and see how big their kids were getting. Over the years while I lived in Olympia, and then even after I moved to Portland, they'd invite me for holiday dinners at Aunt Rita's house, which was next door and connected to their house by way of a back patio and covered walkway. It seemed like a sweet setup, giving Keeva and Kellen daily access to a surrogate seventy-eight-year-old "grandma" (Rita was Hugh's aunt—his late mother's sister).

Even though she was paralyzed on her left side, as a result of a stroke that she'd had years earlier, Rita still lived independently. She drove herself to the store and puttered around her house with the use of a little tripod cane. There were obvious signs that she'd had a stroke, like the big metal brace that was strapped just below her knee and fit into her clunky industrial-looking left shoe, and then there was "lefty," her lifeless hand that would sometimes get hung up in her sleeve as she was dressing. But from her attitude, you'd never know she was mobility-challenged; she was vital, read the paper every day, and would pitch Wiffle balls at Kellen for hours as he stood in her living room.

We'd all pack into Rita's house for dinner and later pull out the playing cards for a rousing game of Boonswaggler, a home-made poker game that involved wearing funny hats and speaking in fake British accents. I never understood the game. I still don't, but it was hilarious, and made me wish my own family was willing to follow up Thanksgiving dinner with a round of stuffy English card-playing, where we'd stick a playing card to our forehead, just below a funny-looking hunting cap, and say, "Tut-tut there, old chap, I don't want to be a bother, but I believe you are bluffing."

Over the past few months, I'd gotten to know Hugh and Annie even better as I traveled up to Olympia for work. We had dinner more often, and they also gently enlisted me to help their friend Mark, who had been diagnosed with lung cancer. It was a challenging time for him, his wife Shelly, and their two young sons, Brett and Kai.

Sometimes we'd do important things such as help organize Mark's pills, a chore that left us sitting around a low coffee table like drug lords, counting and sorting various foul-smelling capsules into tiny Ziploc bags. Other times we did simple tasks: heat the casserole, juice the carrots, wash the dishes, chop wood, stoke the stove, watch Kai practice somersaults on the couch while showing Brett how to make a round paper airplane.

Once, Annie talked me into driving out to Mark and Shelly's house at midnight to secretly placard their yard with signs that said "We Love You" and "Happy Birthday Mark!" I felt like a thirteen-year-old as we sprinted down the long gravel driveway, snickering with our arms full of signs. I had nearly ruptured my spleen holding back a belly laugh when a motion-sensitive light blinked on, surprising us and causing Annie to leap like a fox, pouncing straight up in the air and then dropping down behind one of the smallest shrubs on the planet. God, that was funny.

Another time, Mark asked if we'd help him out to a bonfire pit that was set in a field, four or five hundred feet from the house. Mark wasn't doing well, and couldn't walk on his own, so getting him out to this spot was a bit of a challenge. Someone—probably Hugh—came up with the idea of loading him into a lounge chair, then hefting him in the chair into the back of a truck so we could drive over to the bonfire pit.

It worked! And a half hour later we had a makeshift picnic in the field. Mark leaned back in the lounger, and Brett and Kai saddled up on the armrests to roll into the stick man that was their dad. Shelly sat nearby, while Hugh, Annie, and a few other friends and I sat around on blankets, eating food and watching the clouds float by, forming themselves into castles, chopsticks (not very inventive clouds), and breaking ocean waves. I remember offering, "Oh look, that one looks like a giant baby doll arm. The rest of it should be around here somewhere," which caused us all to furtively search the sky for baby doll legs, hunting for about a nanosecond, until we caught ourselves and started laughing at the weirdness of looking for baby doll body parts in the sky. It was a sweet moment, seeing Mark and Shelly laughing together, doing what normal, cancer-free couples do—what people do when they view the sky like a miracle and there's nothing more fantastic than lounging around under a canopy of clouds with your sweetie.

//////////////////////////

Late at night, as I was driving home to Portland, I'd sometimes think about what I was leaving in Olympia. I'd wonder if I could talk Candyce and Paula into meeting me at the gym the following week, and if they minded (really, sincerely) that I was sleeping in their living room so often. I wondered who was sorting pills at Mark and Shelly's house, which would then send me into how I'd said good-bye—sticking my head into Mark's room and seeing the hospital bed and Hugh beside it, both of them looking at me with a nod and a smile.

I felt connected to Olympia in a new way, and that somehow made the constant highway travel worthwhile; it at least made the monotony worthwhile. Every time I left Olympia to go home, I felt that it had been a good trip.

Things were good, even with the big commute. I felt lucky in the simplest ways, like when I'd search for a parking spot, driving up and down one street and then another, leaning forward into the steering wheel and rubbernecking every ten seconds. Then out of nowhere someone would pull away from the curb, leaving a perfect parking spot.

That's the kind of sheer luck I'd been having lately, but in odd circumstances.

I'd been feeling overly tired, like I was fighting the flu or simply sick of being on the road all the time, and feeling like I needed to sit, lean, rest, relax—and amazingly, perfect resting spots had been showing up out of the blue. In the middle of a walk with my dog, I'd find a set of stairs to sit and catch my breath. At work, as I was standing on a grated platform surrounded by acid baths, I'd find a nearby handrail where I could lean my hip into the metal and rest for a minute while I examined the fire extinguisher mounted on the baluster. I'd relax in my car for a minute, tipping my head back into the headrest after loading groceries into the trunk, sucking in a big breath before cranking the engine to life and carrying on like always.

A few days ago, I went to a bookstore and started to feel weird—so light-headed and sweaty that I went to the bathroom to splash water on my face, only to wake up a few minutes later with my head on the tiles, a store employee was holding my hand and asking if she should call 911. I offered her a sheepish smile and patted her hand, calming her down and explaining that I felt great, even though my heart seemed to be vibrating, purring like I had a cat curled up on the engine block of my chest, a sensation that wasn't painful or uncomfortable, but rather fascinating in the way your front (your tummy and boobs, kneecaps and nose) can be so easily connected to your back (your butt cheeks, shoulder blades, skull, and heels resting on the floor); my whole body vibrated. I didn't think much of it—just figured I needed to take more vitamins, cut back on the coffee, and muscle through it like always, like I'd done a thousand times before . . . but I was wrong.

Torsades

When I was a little girl taking a bath, I would lie back in the tub with my ears underwater. I could hear the air pouring in and out of my lungs, my sister making *wa-wa-wa* talking sounds from the other side of the tub, and the gentle lapping sound of bathwater slushing around my body. Thirty years later, pinched into an exam table in the emergency room, it was much the same. I could hear the nurses making *wa-wa* shouting sounds, hear the space unfold between me and them, and the silence between each blip on the heart monitor. I could feel my heart expanding and contracting, pushing blood up into my ears, polarizing and depolarizing, animating my lungs, firing my brain, bringing me to life just like it should.

My shoes were missing, my arms were tied to the hospital bed, and my chest was exposed to the ceiling. I remember thinking that my boobs looked so small lying there drooping east and west toward the gurney, washed out and nearly disappearing in a sea of electric wires and fluorescent light. My whole body (jaw bone, teeth, soft throat, open airway, rib cage rising and falling, and rising again), my essence, my bearing, and the way I am a loudmouth; my ideas and dreams; my history, lineage, personhood, character, and all of who I imagined I was . . . it was small. The only big thing—the only ginormous, fantastic, real, and over-the-top thing—was the ER nurse's face and the way it seemed to appear out of nowhere to tell me, "Deann . . . Deann . . . Stay with me! You are going to be okay."

"Okay," I puzzled, sounding out the word in my head as if I'd never heard it before, like the nurse was speaking Italian and pretending to know me like my mother, because only my mom would call me Deann.

The day after my foggy dreams in the emergency room, I woke up in an intensive care unit. One of the nurses told me I had fainted and landed there. I'd been resuscitated, once in the ambulance and again in the ER, only to wake up there: lucky and thankful and profoundly confused. The day before (or maybe it was the day before that), I had been a normal, middle-class, middle-of-the-road woman with a mortgage and a job and friends, who went running and climbing and paddling, racing in a thousand different directions at a thousand miles per hour. I was a homeowner who could rewire a bathroom fan, an inspector who had taken a class in "verbal judo" but still got tongue-tied when it came to seeing how nature and some people never really have a chance in life; I was a friend, a sister, a daughter, a wannabe comedian; and now I was a cardiac care patient.

And I was trapped; pinned to the machines that beeped and shooshed all night long, checking blood pressure, respiration, oxygen level, and heart rate. I was tethered to a urine bag and an IV pole, and a heart monitor that seemed to go off every ten minutes, sending a nurse rushing into the room to flick on the fluorescent light, check my IV, and yell, "Deann, you need to keep the cannula in your nose," as she rearranged the plastic tube across my face, behind my ears, and in my nose.

A few days later, I was moved to another room (a sign that I was on the mend), where I could get up to go to the bathroom and order my own meals. I found that the hospital menu confused me with its "heart wise" meals that included coffee and a noodle dish with chipped beef, and then there was the sheer willpower that it took to sit up, organize the various wires, tubes, and electronic gadgets that made reaching for the phone a mystery. It was easier to have them bring whatever food they thought I might like: pudding or red Jell-O cubes, decaffeinated coffee, saltine crackers, meat loaf and mashed potatoes. It was the food they served my grandma at her old folks' home.

Everything was confusing, especially the number of medical people who would walk in and thumb through my chart, then ask me to sit up so they could examine me like a plastic dummy who wouldn't mind a cold stethoscope on her back and under her left breast, then the right; then back to the left, but this time above the areola, squarely over the heart, where the scope would sit for a long time while I listened to the doctor's breath whistle into my ear. There were doctors and interns, two shifts of nurses, phlebotomists, X-ray technicians, a cardiologist, and an electrophysiologist, who seemed to talk right past me.

"You have ventricular tachycardia with torsades," he said, staring at me like I should have a reaction; like I was born with an encyclopedia in my ear and at any moment would reach up, flip to page 864, and know exactly what was going on. "You'll need to make some changes. You won't be able to drive a car for a while, and we'll have to run more tests." I blinked and cocked my head like a spaniel, trying to understand how their commentary fit with what I knew of myself. They continued the discussion, making *wa-wa-wa* talking sounds while I nodded my head in the affirmative. I was lost and assumed that whatever the problem was, the best solution was to leave the hospital as soon as possible. When I asked one of the nurses about that, she said, "Oh, well, we'll see what the doctor thinks."

I was trapped, left conjuring which was the best way to escape—thinking that if I could find some nurse scrubs in the hallway closet, or perhaps convert the IV stand into an axe for tunneling through the floor . . . If I could somehow become someone I'm not then everything would be okay.

My roommate was a lady in her fifties or sixties (actually, I wasn't at all sure of her age, only that she was old enough to have grandkids, and she was sad she couldn't smoke in bed). She was a large lady with a kind, no-nonsense face, reminding me of the cafeteria ladies in grade school—strong women who we all bet could beat up the principal but who would also give you a little wink when you said "Thank you." My roommate would holler over the noise of the television, over the loudness that she had programmed into the TV, to ask me if I was okay. She was maternal. I wasn't. I'd yell back, "Yes. YOU?" secretly praying she wouldn't take the opportunity to talk.

After a few days, when I was feeling more like myself (weak and thin, but me) and like I just wanted to go home, I wandered to her side of the room and asked why she was in the hospital. She went into a long story about cancer and her heart, and then she started crying, sobbing more than any human I've seen, crying about how her boys still needed her even though they were all "growed up," and how she couldn't "go and die" before her second grandbaby was born. I sat on the side of her bed with my hands in my lap, overwhelmed but trying to be sympathetic, as she dug her hands into her eyes like lava was pouring out of them.

The next night, she died.

It was three or four in the morning, and I woke up when one of her monitors started to alarm; and then there was a rush of shoes and more alarms, and a nurse took the curtain that separated us and quickly threw it shut so I couldn't watch how they pulled off her hospital gown and exposed her chest, before yelling, "One, two, three, clear!" They barked orders at one another and yelled "Clear!" half a dozen more times, while I sat on the edge of my bed like a little girl, dangling my feet a few inches from the floor and gripping the edge of the mattress, not breathing, and flinching every time they yelled "Clear!" and hearing her body lift as a jolt of electricity rammed into her rib cage.

Everything grew quiet after that. I took a deep breath and closed my eyes, listening for her raspy breathing, the way she occasionally sent out an enormous *phuft* of breath like a teakettle about to boil over. But all I heard was my own slow heartbeat, banging so hard it made the plastic liner on my bed crinkle, over and over; and it made my head throb, and everything got so hot, my tears dried up before they had a chance to come out of my eyes and the wax in my ears started melting. I sat there for ten, fifteen, then twenty minutes as a steady stream of people came, shuffled around my roommate's bed, and exited. I was waiting. Patient. Wondering how I was supposed to live normally, like always, like an everyday person doing everyday things after this.

I had called my housemates the day before, explaining that I'd fainted at the store near a salad spinner and an onion bin. I made a joke about how the hospital gown made me feel more naked than if I really was naked, and that I was certain the Jell-O cubes were full of wood dust. They told me they were worried, and I'm fairly certain (although I have hardly any memory of it) that I joked around about that too.

Now nothing was funny. I was scared, confused, and angry all at once; so, at any given moment, I wasn't sure how I would react. If the nurse got busy (it was a hospital, after all), I might respond normally with a little joke or at least a smile when she finally popped her head in the room; or, as it happened, I'd react like a freak show . . . so over-the-top frustrated that I imagined I could just rip the IV needle out of my arm, get dressed, and go home.

I stayed. I ate Jell-O and sipped my decaffeinated coffee, which tasted exactly like warm black water with a splash of something resembling what I remembered as "coffee"—a trick, a concoction that plays with your mind, like maybe real coffee wasn't as great as you once thought. They seemed to do this with all the food.

I was released with various heart medications and a promise that I would be evaluated in another couple of weeks to see how things were going. John, my housemate, picked me up and we immediately drove to a burger joint, gripping the curbs like an ambulance, so I could order a chocolate milk shake. It was perfect, and John was perfect. The car was perfect, and the way the sun filtered through the clouds and made the seat belt buckles glisten . . . that was perfect.

And when we got home, I realized the house was perfect

too—even with the front porch steps tilting a little left, and with the drafty windows that we'd sealed up with plastic for the winter making the house look like it was squinting (ogling its way past filmy Coke-bottle glasses). It was inviting and warm, and as I walked in, I took a deep, overly exaggerated breath, the sort of over-the-top gesture that was filmed for commercials about scented laundry detergent, but in this case was my way of trying to absorb every molecule of my old normal life. I loved the smell of the living room, the kitchen, Jenna's recycling porch, the cupboards, and the basement laundry room. I loved everything, and it seemed to love me back. It was as if my heart had grown to three times its normal size, and it could now hold the specialness of every person who crossed my path; it could track how phenomenal every scent, sound, taste, or texture was. Everything was beautiful, even if it was just the laundry that I'd pulled out of the dryer, still warm, and hugged like a small, lost child.

Over the next few weeks, things continued to be weird. I fainted and got sweaty, and felt that rumbling vibration in my chest far more often than I like to admit. It was as if my heart was weathering a storm, a tornado blowing out transformers and knocking the windows, just like the tornados I saw as a kid growing up in the Midwest.

When I was a junior in high school, a small tornado hit Liberty, Missouri—the town located a few miles from our family's farm. The day after, my friends and I drove around in a stupor, looking at the damage: cars flipped over like toys, like someone had picked them up and simply turned them upside down in their parking spot. There was a horse in a tree, and the oaks and elms near the junior high school had been stripped of their leaves and now looked like a collection of giant pitchforks. It was horrifying, and then there were the unbelievable-but-true stories we heard: how one family was in the middle of a birthday party, sitting at the dinner table, when they heard the tornado sirens in town. They had just enough time to race into the bathroom, where all four of them lay like sardines in the bathtub as the wind invaded their house. In the kitchen, the tornado opened cabinets, threw dinner plates, and smashed canned goods into the dishwasher. It snatched spoons and forks off the table and shot them through the walls, and launched the roast chicken like a wrecking ball into the ceiling. Minutes later, when the family finally crawled out, thankful to be alive and happy to see their house still standing, they found the kitchen looking like a bomb had gone off, but—this was the weird part—the birthday cake that had been sitting in the middle of the kitchen table was perfectly fine. They found it still sitting in the same spot, without so much as a finger-dab in the frosting.

My cardiac problems were confused like that: like a horse in a tree and a surviving cake. And I needed to feel less wonky in the world; I needed to feel like me.

I threw myself into my routine—walking the dog, making

dinner, racing to work, paying the mortgage and bills. I happily hid behind the chaos of each day, and then alone at night I thought about what had happened and what was happening. I kept replaying that feeling of waking up in the hospital, of seeing the nurses race through a series of moves, setting IVs and prepping me for the next series of moves. It felt like death, or my mortality, or something bigger still, was leaning into my bed with the moonlight, clattering when I moved hangers in the closet, buzzing behind the sound of the shower running or my car idling in traffic. The wall that kept opposites in place—life, death, me, others, lucky or not—had been toppled; nothing made sense anymore.

I sat in the kitchen one day after buying a bag of clothespins, a simple task, engineered so I could dry my laundry in the basement near the hot furnace, and then months later in the summer sun. As I was pouring them onto the kitchen table, I realized the technical genius in this simple tool. Perfectly shaped wood pinchers and a dime-size metal spring that creates just enough tension to hold a pair of pants on a clothesline—there must be a dozen patents assigned to clothespins. I looked a bit closer, and without much imagination at all, I could see birch trees growing in a forest, gathering sun (having a life), when all of a sudden everything shifted. The trees were cut down and rolled through a mill, and turned into a million three-inch pinchers with precise quality-controlled diameters, lengths, weights, and future function. Meanwhile, on the other side of the planet, iron ore was being blasted out of the ground, then melted and extruded and formed into long bits of wire that were eventually twisted into the springs that were shipped half-way around the world to a factory where they could be joined to the wood pinchers to make clothespins. And all the while, on both sides of the planet, there were any number of human workers (having a life) being paid pennies a day to run the machines or to hand-count the clothespins, bundling them into bags and inventorying them into boxes that were then loaded into crates to be sent by barge to America so good environmental stewards and penny-pinchers like me could pin up their clothes in the sun.

I didn't know how to respond to that, so I set the bag aside and took my dog for a walk.

A Moment of Genius
While Waiting

A month later, I returned to the hospital for an echocardio-gram—an ultrasound that takes a movie of your heart much like the sonogram I'd get if I were pregnant, awaiting the first tiny snapshot of my peanut baby with flipper arms that I would show all my friends and coworkers. It was like that, but no one would send me home with a photo of my heart. Instead, they'd send me home with news about how well my body would work, and for how much longer. By now, I'd come to trust my cardiologist and understood that he was trying the best he could to help me, to get me running again (literally), and to see me do more than scrape by; he wanted me to thrive. He was the kind of man who laughed a lot—probably the sort who often cried or peed his pants while laughing (my personal favorite). I trusted him, completely.

I was waiting for my turn, thumbing through magazines, trying to ignore how all the people around me were ten thousand years old, and how, like them, I had a ten-thousand-year-old's cardiac problems, when I came across an article about a guy who'd built a tiny house on wheels, a house smaller than my garage, smaller than a parking spot. It looked like a cabin that would be used in a commercial for pancake batter, or in a painting titled *A Simpler Time*.

The article indicated that the owner had built the house himself, a fact that caused me to pull the magazine closer so I could examine the guy's arms. To my surprise, they didn't appear to be overly manly or even any stronger than my own. The article went on to explain that he had built the little house and then moved it to a spot behind his bigger, 1,200-square-foot house, tucking it near a low fence and scrub oak tree.

I was curious about Tiny House Man. Apparently, he rented out the big house and lived "for free" in the backyard, while his renters paid the mortgage and utilities. No bills. No overwhelming debt. A house the size of a Tic Tac to clean.

Suddenly, a light went on. Literally: a flashing red light. There was an emergency code somewhere in the bowels of the hospital, and as the lights flashed, my cardiologist fled down the hall, and I was left sitting there with the tiny-house article for an hour. I just stared at it, mulled it over, daydreamed, and then thought: What would happen if I just . . . sort of . . . did that?

What if I sold my big house with its rats in the front yard, the mortgage, the hours of dusting, mopping, cleaning, vacuuming, painting, grass cutting, and yard pruning? How would it feel to live so light?

I wasn't sure why I was so drawn to the photo, but the best I could figure was that it reminded me of everything I'd wanted as an eight-year-old, when I'd have been happy living in a tree stump or a tree house, or even in the scratchy little caves that my brothers and I carved out of the blackberry bushes along the fence line of our farm. The point was that I'd have a place of my own where I could hide from my chores or my family, where I could cry my eyes out if I needed to and make sense of the world by viewing it through a tiny spyhole. I had big plans for myself: I'd live in the woods and learn to speak to the chipmunks and squirrels. I'd spend my time examining the small bones and rocks found in the nearby creek bed. I'd make "sit-upons," leafy sort of seat cushions, just like we did in Girl Scouts, and whittle tiny stick figures for my mother. I'd do whatever I wanted, whenever I wanted, and in the end, all the woodland creatures would become my best friends forever, but for even longer. *That* was my dream life, so perhaps you can understand why the idea of building a tiny wooden house would click for me. Plus, building a house would be fun!

Then there was another voice. The idea of living in a tiny

wood house appealed to my inner eight-year-old, but what kind of adult does that? I wondered if Tiny House Man was happy; if he had good friends who would come over for dinner despite the cramped quarters, if they packed themselves into the living room (which was also the kitchen and bathroom), where they'd balance their dinner plates on their laps and play mini Scrabble with tiles the size of their teeth. I wondered if he had lumps on his head from sitting up in the night and smashing into the ceiling. Was Tiny House Man dogged by his decision to live so small, perhaps shunned by his neighbors, who secretly joked about his house; or did people love that he had downsized himself into the equivalent of a toolshed?

I wondered what kind of man would choose to live in a house that small when he obviously had other options. He didn't live in Ireland, where a person might build a little Hobbit hut and live happy as a wee elf. This wasn't Mongolia, Africa, South America, or China, where people regularly lived in houses that were barely big enough to keep the sun and rain off your head; this was America, where everything is BIG.

Maybe Tiny House Man was ill, suffering from a mental disorder that made it impossible to make wise decisions, like Ted Kaczynski (the man who made shoe-box-size bombs and mailed them out all over the country), who ended up pleading insanity, using the small size of his cabin and the fact that it didn't have running water as proof of his problems. I thought about what might constitute normal or normal-ish behavior, wise and not-so-wise decisions, and ultimately, I hoped the tiny-house guy was similar to me: a sane person without a big agenda, who simply wanted a way to make sense of the world, to create a new map with a big X in the middle labeled "Home," even if that meant shrinking his world down to the size of an area rug.

My life was normal (or at least, normal-ish), though my new diagnosis and machinery made me feel chaotic inside. Before leaving the hospital, I had a defibrillator implanted—a gadget that would normally be delivered in a suitcase to the side of an ailing patient, but in my case was all sewn in, corkscrewed into my heart and wired to a battery that floated in my belly. It worked like this: If my heart rate suddenly spiked, causing me to pass out, the box (as I called it) would deliver a jolt of electricity to send me flying forward like I'd been donkey-kicked in the ass. It was like being Tasered from the inside out. My friends and I joked that I was the only one of us who could likely jump-start a car by running in place, or who could reasonably ask her lover to wear rubber boots connected to a grounding wire. We joked about it; but it unnerved me.

I never knew when my heart would quit and my defibrillator would fire. My doctors and I couldn't connect it to the food I ate, water, beer, sex, vitamin deficiency, exercise, anxiety, thyroid problems, stress, joy, monotony, my job, scary movies, or the number of times I'd shot myself off a ladder doing home improvement projects. There wasn't any specific behavior that triggered my weird heart rhythm; it was a mystery, and that left me feeling lost inside.

One week, in spite of all advice to the contrary, I went for a run; three miles, up to the top of Mount Tabor and back. I wanted to test my heart, challenge it to see if it would explode like a water balloon in my chest or simply stop, like releasing a doorknob after you walk in the house. I raced up to my house and doubled over with my hands on my knees, like I always do, expecting to crumple into a wad of fluff on the porch. But nothing happened. I was fine.

And then two days later, as I sat at my desk, writing a report, my heart seized. It was like a switch was thrown, like the *pffft* out of a wall socket when the fuse pops; I nearly fainted, but instead I drove myself (against all reason) to the urgent care facility.

My heart made me see everything different, like looking at your over-sized legs dangling inside the water at the edge of a pool. I found myself stalled out at the grocery store, ogling the rows of produce, dishes, pots, scrub brushes, and soup ladles, imagining the people who may have spent their life propagating, harvesting, designing, and building these genius goods; items that were now a dime a dozen, expected, disposable, forgettable. I found myself staring out the window at the birds and the clouds, at the way rain gathered into tiny river deltas near the base of the windowpane. One day I started crying at a stoplight because the red color was so brilliantly beautiful, and the idea of stoplights so perfect in a civil society. Later, I had an epiphany while trying to fix the vacuum cleaner, bending over it with a pair of pliers, with little parts fanned out on the rug all around me. I thought: *This* is what the living do. And I swooned at the ordinary nature of the task and myself, at my chapped hands and square palms, at the way my wrists bent and fingers flexed inside this living body.

Another day, I found myself telling a city inspector, a complete stranger, everything about my life. He had come to the house to evaluate why rats had burrowed into a hole in the front yard, and why they refused to leave even though I had purchased something called the "sonic emitter"—a contraption that was supposed to produce a high-frequency noise, inaudible to humans but ear-splitting to rats and guaranteed to send all varmints packing.

The inspector spoke with a southern drawl and wore an orange safety vest that made him look like a traffic cone. He explained the serious nature of pest control and how some people "just don't give a fiddle-faddle," and how he once saw rat turds in a silverware drawer but didn't say anything to the homeowners because they "weren't the sorts to take a note on it anyways." And then, for some undefined reason (some bizarre, oddly satisfying reason), I told him the story about how I'd just gotten out of the hospital, and how I felt like I was walking around with a hole in me that every living thing seemed to fall into. He gave me a little tap on the hand as he handed off the inspection report and pointed to his listed recommendations. "Change what you can, darlin'. That's my best advice."

I remember thinking: What would I change? That's easy. I'd be on a perpetual vacation where I'd swim with dolphins and eat mangos every day, and I wouldn't have to work or pay a mortgage. I'd travel to stunning, wild places; visit my family, and hang out with my friends and let their toddlers put cereal in my hair, cry in my arms, and poop in my lap—not because I like poop but because that is exactly the sort of real-life stuff I would want to have in the mix. I'd walk the Pacific Crest Trail from the Mexican border to Canada if my heart could handle it, which led me to what I really wanted to change: me. My heart. If I could change anything, I wanted to *not* think about my heart every five minutes. I wanted to have the nurses stop scribbling "congestive heart failure" in my medical chart, and I wanted to quit imagining that I was dying a little bit every day. I wanted to stop looking at everything so intensely—studying my housemates, the neighbors, my friends, the clouds, the way the sun warms me like it's filling in the cavities between each and every one of my 4 trillion living cells. I wanted to stop looking at everything and thinking how perfect it is, and how much I was going to miss it, and then feeling so sad because I didn't want to miss anything.

As I sat there in the waiting room, waiting for the next round of diagnoses, the idea of building a tiny house seemed to make all the sense in the world. Somehow, it would shrink my life into a manageable mouthful and connect me to the trouble-free kid who raced around her backyard catching fireflies at night.

And building would be fantastic—a monumental project that would absorb every brain cell, and every ounce of focus and ability, and then maybe I'd stop staring at the sun like the most stunning act of God ever imagined. It would put all my home repair and remodeling skills to the test, and I'd have a chance to build something perfect; something warm and kind, and made out of materials that didn't make me feel like I was lying to myself every time I claimed to be an environmentalist. I could build a little house like Tiny House Man, and if it made sense, I might even be able to move into it and let go of my big house—a move that would entail letting go of the perfect back-yard, the beautiful gardens, and the accommodating floor plan, along with the mortgage, the utility bills, and the hours spent laboring to keep things from falling under the weight of time and the elements. Maybe I could walk away from all that. Maybe.

Deciding that I needed to take some kind of action, I tore the article out of the magazine and smuggled it out under my shirt like porn. When I got home, I stuck the picture on the refrigerator, and for the next week, every time I caught a glimpse of the pointy little roof, I'd get happy-melty feelings.

I convinced myself that I needed to find Tiny House Man. It was a completely logical course of action, like tracking down Jonas Salk for more information about his polio vaccine, or finding the manufacturers of a particular product to see if there were any small pieces that presented a choking hazard. I needed to know the details, and a week after staring at the Tiny House Man and his perfect creation a thousand different times, studying the magazine photo in the same way a jewel thief would ogle the Queen's crown, I decided to call directory assistance in Iowa City—that's where the article placed Jay Shafer, The Tiny House Man.

My hands started sweating as I stood in my kitchen, then paced from the oven to the kitchen sink, holding the phone, and then dialed the operator in Iowa City and asked for Jay Shafer. A moment later, she offered me his phone number. Just like that, I had the winning lottery ticket. I simultaneously wanted to barf and scream. I grabbed RooDee and went for a walk, talking to myself along the way: "Hello, Jay Shafer, this is Dee Williams and I wanted to . . . I was hoping that . . . I like your house and . . . your house is really cool and . . . I want to . . . *hope* to . . . build one too." So it went for a half an hour, then an hour as I worked my way through the neighborhood, up and down the same street over and over, trying to find the right way to ask Jay for help. I stood in my kitchen like I did when I was stealing myself for an inspection, tucking my hair behind my ears and standing up straight, chest out . . . like a lion tamer ready to invite his opponent out of its cage. "Hello, Jay," I boomed in a false bravado, "How you doing today?"

In the long run, five minutes after I hung up the phone, I

couldn't remember what we had said, or how the conversation had played out. I had asked him a few questions about the house, what it cost and how long it took to make, and then we had made a tentative plan to get together if I ever came to town. We had laughed a lot, and I'd hung up incredibly satisfied with myself. And then I bought a plane ticket.

Tiny House Man

I am not a graceful traveler. I am frenetic. I constantly search my pockets for my boarding pass. I give myself a little pat-down as I stand in line at the security gate, and then again as I race from one monitor to the next, where I mumble the gate number and my brain goes *ding* like an oven timer, and I check for my boarding pass again. I was particularly goofy en route to Iowa, and left my wallet in the bathroom, which meant I had to trek back through the terminal, around suitcases and wheel-chairs, and past annoying people wearing smug "I know exactly where my boarding pass is" looks and irritating people bottlenecking the corridor, making it nearly impossible for me to get to my wallet, which, as it turned out, was in my hand the whole time.

The truth was, regardless of my usual worries, I was incredibly nervous about meeting Tiny House Man, and I wasn't sure why. I had called my brother Doug, who also happened to live in Iowa City. I explained why I wanted to visit, and he had purred little questions into the phone like a therapist. "So you want to find the Tiny House Man and build a tiny house?"

"Yes." I curled my arms reflexively over my head and cradled the phone to my ear, wondering what Doug was thinking. Did he think I was crazy, behaving irrationally, or headed for some terrible crash landing?

"Okay," he whispered back. "We always seem to figure it out."

So, just like that, I had enlisted my brother. I explained that Jay had invited me to come visit, and Doug was game for the adventure.

Growing up on our farm, Doug had been my accomplice in a number of backyard experiments and building projects. We built hay forts and made hidey-holes, and crawled through the attic looking for treasure. We caught tadpoles and fireflies, and lay out on hay bales, staring at the sky, daydreaming about the candy we would buy (M&M's, Jujubes, or chocolate bars) when we were "old and rich."

As the eldest sibling, I was typically the instigator of our shenanigans, suggesting for example that we make a catapult to throw each other across the yard. Doug, who was nearly as big as me even though he was five years younger, would usually team with me to take care of business, to (for example) work with me to bend a tree sapling into a tight U-shape as a perfect catapult or slingshot. We would then usually enlist our younger brother, Mark, to support our brilliant ideas, asking him to sit at the whip end of the tree (again for example) with a soup kettle on his head for protection. In the case of the catapult, we were ultimately foiled; the thing didn't shoot straight because the physics were off (Mark was too heavy, he wouldn't sit right, and he appeared to be crying), and besides, the tree was too scratchy and my mom screamed when she saw what we were doing.

Another time, my brothers and I convinced ourselves we were kung fu masters. I still have a lump on my leg from the day I attempted a complicated ninja move from the barn loft, where I had tied an extension cord (the closest thing I could find to a rope) to a rafter near the peak of the roof. I figured I could swing out the second-story window, turn around in midair, and fly right back into the barn, where I'd land catlike on the floor, somersault, and come up with my hands poised in a karate chop. I imagined this would be my coolest trick ever, and I think I yelled "Hey, watch this!" to my brothers as I grabbed the cord, took a running leap, and shot myself out the window into the blank airspace above the cows.

Moments into the ride, I felt the rubber cord stretch with my weight, and the knot loosening as I hit the farthest point on my swing. I flailed my legs and twisted around, and that's when I knew I was in trouble. I came back at the building, knees first, scraped along the barn wall, and dropped eight feet into the barnyard manure, where I lay conscious but unmoving, trying to assess the damage to my legs, my ninja pride, and the damaged extension cord (which my dad would later shake his head over and spank me for ruining). Meanwhile, my brothers thought this was the funniest thing they'd ever seen: "Just like a cartoon!" they cried. "Do it again!"

Doug became a Methodist minister, a vocation that complemented his ability to witness people do dumb shit and then help them pick up the pieces. He had recently flown to Portland to be with me after my defibrillator was implanted. I woke up in the cardiac care unit to find him sleeping next to me; he'd stayed up all night listening to the heart monitor, and had finally dozed off in a nearby chair. When he woke up, he found his "ass crack on backward," so he'd crawled up on the bed beside me, lying on his back. He had dangled his legs off the bed to avoid accidentally bumping my bubble-packed chest and the sea of associated tubes and wires, and then crossed his arm over his torso so he could tuck his right hand into his left pants pocket, leaving him looking like a leaf of wilted lettuce. He looked "here but gone," which was just how I felt.

Everyone needs a good accomplice, and in some weird way, I knew finding the Tiny House Man in Iowa City was a good thing—like divinity or fate was working in our favor—simply by the fact that Jay lived in the same town as my brother Doug.

Jay's house was in a residential neighborhood, tucked

behind a larger normal house, and as we walked to the backyard, we found him standing on his porch, waiting for us, looking incredibly large given the small scale of his abode. I found myself approaching him with a mixture of complete excitement and hesitating fear . . . like a four-year-old seeing Santa at the mall. I was too nervous to say anything funny or weird, and instead smiled and shook his outreached hand and mumbled, "I have a photo of you and your house stuck to my refrigerator," which instantly made me feel like a miniature copy of that article was stuck in my teeth.

"Doesn't everyone?" he said, putting his hands on his hips in a Superman pose and looking off in the distance like a statue. Apparently, his sense of humor was on par with mine; I immediately liked him.

Before we went inside, while Doug and Jay talked on the porch, I walked around the house, gunning my hand along the siding and patting the window sashes. I loved Jay's little house and found myself wanting to hug it, to lean into it and smell it or get my picture taken next to it like I was standing with the president. Inside, Jay gave us a short tour (a little joke at the time) and then we sat down around a tiny table with our knees touching. It felt like the sort of thing you'd do at a noisy café, where you'd naturally scoot in to hear each other and accidentally touch toes or kick each other when you crossed your legs. Jay pulled out a wad of papers and photographs, spreading them out on the small table between us, and then showed us floor plans and elevations, construction details, and sketches of some of the other houses he had designed. He and Doug chit-chatted about how the house was connected to the trailer and how the walls were reinforced, and all the while I was mostly quiet. I glanced around at the knotty pine walls, the kitchen setup with its shiny galley sink and stainless steel countertop, and the way the cabinets were joined together. I casually cocked my head, trying not to seem overly nosy as I read the titles of books stacked on the shelves—books about cabins, barns, tree houses, yurts, converted vans, an "Earthship," old hippie wagons, shepherds' wagons, chuck wagons, hay wagons, boats, and old Airstreams. His bookshelves looked like an expanded version of my own, and like my favorite part of the local bookstore where I'd spent hours in the past month crouched on a movable step stool, pouring through books; sitting there till someone tapped me on the shoulder, telling me it was closing time and I might as well collect all the books and just put them on the nearby stack table so an employee could reshelve them later.

Jay wanted to know why I was interested in building. I hesitated for a second and then joked, "I want a house that goes with my squirrel costume." I didn't want to talk about the real reasons, about my mortgage and the way I was tired of working all the time, or about my heart stuff, which was way too personal and private, and far too confused for polite conversation.

He smiled and gave me an uncomfortable look. I *knew* that look; it was the way I sometimes stared at someone when I thought they were holding something back. It was an intuitive thing, where you get a sense there's more to the story, and it was also something that I'd refined through work. I'd learned how to watch a person's eyes to see if they looked up and to the left like they're accessing a seldom-used part of their brain, which would be their imagination and a sign that they were lying. So, as I was sitting there with Jay Shafer, as I looked up and to the left and made my little joke about squirrels, I realized I wanted to come clean; I at least wanted to offer more of the truth, even if I couldn't offer all of it.

I launched into a story about a trip that Doug and I had taken to Guatemala the year before and the impact it had on me; how I'd gotten to see how most of the world really lives: without running water or a decent toilet. I explained that I felt like a cliché in Guatemala, like a typical wealthy American tourist speaking English to the locals and pantomiming when that failed, wandering around with a fanny pack and a floppy hat, feeling nervous about getting dysentery or being robbed. "The people there," I explained, "are constantly crapping their pants with preventable diseases."

I went to Guatemala to help build a school but left wondering what "help" would really look like. Many of them lived without electricity or access to medical care. They lived with the memory of a civil war; a war that included babies being ripped out of their mothers' arms and thrown into the forests like cordwood, as a priest had described one day. Even the little town where we were working, a town smaller than the ten square blocks that made up my neighborhood, was under curfew with barricades in the street and *policía* patrolling at night. The people I worked with and met were great; they barely had enough food to eat but always offered to share what they had; and even though I hadn't ever experienced a war and poverty, or what it felt like to watch a child die from diarrhea, they never for a minute treated me like a spoiled white lady. I hadn't prepared myself for how humbled I'd feel, or how hard it would be to find my footing when witnessing a cycle of poverty that seemed to defy any sort of help.

Doug chimed in and, together, we positively gushed about Guatemala—how spider monkeys walk like old men with artificial hips and bowed legs; how there are more butterflies and banana trees than coffee beans, and how the kids play soccer like the pros. I explained that the trip had challenged my interest in continuing to pump money into my house, paying four-hundred dollars for wood trim along the ceiling in the living room because, according to my logic, "it would really pull the room together."

It was a compelling explanation for wanting to give up my big house and build a tiny house. And it was completely true, but so was the unstated fact that I was a bit lost with my heart.

I didn't know what to do with the way my heart problems had become so predominant in my life—the way I felt my mortality just as clearly as I felt my vitality. It's hard to explain why you love the morning sunlight because it proves you too are a miracle for waking up.

It's not exactly the story you offer to a stranger.

Doug asked me about Guatemala as we were driving home; it was the first time I'd talked about the trip this way, and he was curious. "Well," I explained, "there was no way that he would believe that story about the squirrel costume."

Later that night, I tried to describe Jay's house to Doug's wife, Alecia. I talked about the cedar siding and the woodstove, and the way you could pop into the sleeping loft through a little cubbyhole near the kitchen. I explained how the space felt small but not claustrophobic, simple but not crude, and functional in that everything had a purpose and a place. I talked and talked, describing this detail and that feature, but ultimately, Jay's house was more than all those things. It was bigger.

The house reminded me of the road trip I had taken when I was in my twenties: I wanted to leave the Midwest permanently but couldn't just yet, so I recruited some friends to drive with me to Colorado for a weekend in the mountains. We left Kansas City after dinner and drove all night across the Great Plains with nothing but the moon and the idea that if we kept switching channels, we might find something better on the radio.

We drove until we finally hit Boulder, where we stopped at a Get N Go gas station with a sign that emphasized GO, but suddenly all we wanted was to stay, because as soon as we opened our car doors, as we stepped out into the predawn cold and let the mountain air hit us, the pine tree pitch settled into our arms and we realized . . . we had arrived. We could finally stop all our rushing and let the smell of the forest—now mere inches from our fingertips and still hidden in the early-morning shadows off the highway—settle into our lungs. Everyone was quiet, happy, suspended in the moment, with one foot still resting in the car and a hand still holding the door latch.

Jay's house was like that.

Doug and I spent the next couple of days planning, talking about the trailer configuration and walls, yammering through dinner and while we were out walking the farm, as he showed me the place where he sometimes found morel mushrooms and the spot where his goats kept chewing through the fence. We tried to pin down how long it would take to build a house similar to Jay's, and I estimated two or three weeks—the same amount of time it had previously taken me to build a short ramp (a single piece of wood) for a friend's cat to enter and exit through the cat door. Doug figured it would take longer, but I was so excited to see the final product that I completely ignored his more realistic calculations.

On the plane ride home, I doodled little floor plans, dreaming about where I'd sleep and cook, and how I'd build the floors and walls. I imagined how the door would open and I would walk into a place that felt like home, whatever that meant, however that played out.

I imagined that my house would be modeled after Jay's but different: It would be roughly the same size, set on a trailer, then I'd build an open front porch where you could lounge like you were having a tailgate party, and a kitchen and living room that would open up through skylight windows, like walking into an empty barn with light pouring in through the cupolas. Simple. Kind. And as E. B. White said in *Charlotte's Web*, "like nothing bad could ever happen again."

Now all I had to do was take my own bait, to convince myself that I could do this! It felt like a big commitment; the trailer alone would cost nearly $2,000, so if I was going to walk into a metal shop and have them start welding away, I needed to know I was serious. Then there was the little matter of my heart. Perhaps the current state of my health should have raised a bright red caution flag, but instead it fired me up. I wanted to do what *I* wanted. I didn't care if hefting plywood and climbing a ladder weren't on my doctor's recommended list of activities, or if I was foolhardy to think I could lift a fifty-pound roll of tar paper into and then out of my car. I was going to do it because it sounded like a blast, like the best possible way to have fun. It sounded akin to hiking into bear country with nothing but a backpack, my wits, and a one-pound bag of mini Snickers bars (which everyone knows is a backpacking essential). Building my own house sounded like something Laura Ingalls Wilder would have done if she hadn't been trapped in that gingham dress and lived under the shadow of her nickname, "Half-Pint."

I thought of building my own house as the greatest adventure a girl could have. And that was that.

As fate would have it, I arrived home and found a set of house plans curled in a cardboard tube, waiting for me in a stack of mail; Jay had already sent them with a little congratulatory note and a double-dog dare to "go for it!"

Fear and Logic

(OLYMPIA, WASHINGTON, APRIL 2012)

No one comes to visit me without calling first. They are afraid to walk past the gate, then down my friends' driveway, past their house and into the backyard where my little house sits. They stand out by the mailbox, worrying how to best trespass beyond the big house to the little house without being seen; or they scheme how to walk through, singing "Yoo-hooo" to minimize any alarm. It's a lot to think about, so my friends usually call first.

Given all of that, you can understand my surprise when earlier today, my friend Dave knocked on the door without calling first, wanting to know if I would help him pick up a wood chipper from a rental store. Dave is the sort of guy who doesn't ask for help, so when he does, it makes you feel like a champion, like you're donating blood or delivering medicine to an isolated village. Still, it was raining, and I was curious about why today was the day, but agreed all the same simply because I was super-curious about the chipper.

If you're not familiar with a chipper, it is a giant version of the garbage disposal that sits below a kitchen sink, or a giant version of your own small mouth, wherein tree branches are shoved in, chopped into thumb-size pieces, and spit out the back of the unit. We went to the rental place and hitched the chipper to my truck, then drove to Dave's house. He had recently pruned several fruit trees, along with fir and spruce trees, and hoped to grind down the remnants into usable compost. This is what people do in early spring when they tidy up; they look around the yard after a few months of hiding indoors, wondering how badly the winter wind, snow, and rain have mangled their yard, and they see that things are mostly okay but perhaps in need of some pruning. And so they rent a chipper.

I have a lot of power tools, but nothing compares to a chipper, the workhorse of destructive behavior. The unit came with a long liability waiver and a four-page pamphlet with intimidating precautions, telling us to wear safety glasses and hearing protection, and to avoid horsing around and being sucked into the unit. Neither of us had ever operated a chipper, so we hesitantly started by shoving thin twigs into the hopper (the mouth of the unit) and watching them explode out the back in a satisfying array of brown and green; this was followed by Dave and me giving each other the thumbs-up and graduating to slightly larger branches.

As we worked, we got more comfortable but never completely relaxed with the way the chipper would quickly grab the branches and then automatically suck it into its gullet like a four-year-old slurping spaghetti noodles. Even Dave, a manly man who in another life would likely have worn beaver pelts and carried an axe everywhere he went, would instinctively pull his head back and scrunch up his face as if the unit might projectile-vomit at any moment.

We each wore red clamshell protection over our ears, which reduced our communication to a series of pantomimed gestures. At one point, I'd signaled Dave to "watch this" by wiggling two fingers in front of my eyes and flipping them toward the hopper, and then I shoved an unbelievably large branch (nearly the size of a Christmas tree) into the unit. It sprayed out the back like confetti shot out of a cannon, making us hoot. In response, Dave grabbed an even larger branch and shot it through the unit. Next, he bit the top off a pinecone like he was pulling the pin on a grenade and lobbed it into the hopper. He grabbed a plastic pop bottle and threw that in the chipper too, and while his wife was watching, he dragged a lawn chair over and pretended he was going to shove that through the unit.

The sun came out and we threw all sorts of crap into the chipper: rotten lumber, an old rubber boot (because we could, though we later discovered it was a pain in the buttocks to remove the little rubber bits from the compost), crappy wood planters, cedar shakes, and tree limbs. We finished up, staggering around the chip pile sprayed out on the lawn; feeling satisfied and slightly dizzy when we finally pulled off our earmuffs. "That kicked ass," I yelled.

Operating a chipper is the sort of behavior that makes me feel like a gladiator, like I'm larger than I am—taller and more capable. It's also nice because it's so easy to see that you've accomplished something monumental at the end of the day—where you once had a giant mishmash of tree limbs, branches, and brambles, now you had a tidy pile of usable wood chips. Just like that. Voilà: Success.

The other (perhaps less reasonable) reason I appreciated operating the chipper is because it scared the piss out of me. When I first started shoving stuff into the blades, I got a little zing in the pants and my kneecaps quivered. And actually, even before we left the rental store, before I pushed the first tiny stick into the chipper, I was afraid I could lose an eye. I worried that something would malfunction, that we'd miss a step, overlook a risk, or otherwise slip on the proverbial banana peel and end up as viscera in the mulch pile. At Dave's house, I confronted those fears reasonably well by using my fourteen-pound head. Fear and logic belong together. I reread the precautions and thought ahead to what could go wrong, and I reevaluated how to best get my body and brain to work together. Finally, I put on my goggles, hearing protection, and toughest set of nerves, and went to work. We opened up a big ol' can of whoop-ass, and *that* was an exhilarating feeling.

////////////////////////

In the few months since I had returned from Iowa, I had vacillated between outright panic and resting comfortably in the notion that I could figure things out. Every time I'd look at my blueprints, I felt like a member of the Lewis and Clark expedition, where instead of planning to map rivers, mountain meadows, and the curious habits of the local residents, I'd be navigating the grizzled, manly world of carpentry.

The thing that scared me the most was the idea of moving the little house down the highway. I'd seen plenty of evidence along the highway to confirm that people don't know jack about hauling stuff. In a single trip down a fifteen-mile stretch of the interstate, I counted a dozen things that had likely blown out of trucks at high speed: a mattress, a sofa (minus the cushions, but I saw those a couple of miles later), a cat-scratch tower, a dinner table, smashed-up plastic lawn chairs, and what appeared to be a bicycle folded in half. I felt sad about each item, and worried over the people who were likely crying about their orphaned shoes and missing barbecue grill.

I didn't want that to happen to me, so I started examining my options for keeping the house from suddenly veering sideways whenever a massive semitruck passed. I wanted to stop it from lunging forward when I threw on the brakes, or sliding backward into a nosedive on the pavement like the coffee cup that I'd recently left on the roof of my car (the cup actually hung in there for several miles before losing its grip and bouncing on the car bumper on its way down).

Jay had already figured out what was required by the Department of Motor Vehicles to be safe: I had to build the house short enough to slide under highway overpasses, and skinny enough to avoid bloating a single traffic lane. I wasn't sure which state trooper invented the numbers, but I wasn't going to mess with the math or fudge the measurements; my house would be no more than thirteen and a half feet tall, and eight and a half feet wide.

Securing the house to the trailer was a bit more of a head-scratcher. Jay had constructed the floor of his house above the trailer, like strapping a couch to a skateboard to move it across town. He'd used a thousand screws to secure the wood floor frame to the metal trailer frame, but I wanted something different. I wanted the floor to fit inside the metal trailer, like putting your foot in a ski boot, so the two components would work intrinsically as one.

I went to the library and researched how other people had done this; I looked at gypsy wagons, covered wagons, travel trailers, and RVs, and poked around trying to find specific references on how to secure a boat to a trailer, and how those cute little garden sheds at the lumberyard were moved when they were sold. There wasn't anything that I could find that was an exact match. Travel trailers were made out of lightweight aluminum and plastic; shepherds' wagons were lightweight wood and canvas; while my house would be made out of thousands of pounds of lumber, plywood, and metal.

I needed something different, and I figured that if I could decipher how a carpenter might build a normal, wooden house along a fault line, in an area where earthquakes happen all the time, then I'd have a good idea of how to build my house to handle the gyrating bumps, jolts, and vibration of the highway. The same logic applied to high winds and driving rain; I just had to discover how houses were built to withstand a hurricane.

"I don't have to reinvent the wheel," I told my brother when we were talking on the phone one day, "just modify it." Which is how I found myself sitting at the library with a small mountain of notebooks containing what was quite possibly the most boring literature in the world: the City of Seattle and City of Portland building codes.

Both cities have plenty of wood structures sitting above what they call the Pacific Ring of Fire, an earthquake-prone geography riddled with active volcanoes. I remember climbing one of those volcanoes, Mount Hood, in February one year. Everything was draped in snow, and the topography took on a lumpy mashed-potato quality with cartoonish rocky outcrops and puckered ice at the crevasse edges. Our route took us to the lip of the caldera, the mouth of the volcano, where we could see steam vents cracking the surface of the snow. As we were hiking, we'd occasionally smell the sulfur farting out of the earth—an odor that I first thought was coming from Steve-o, my climbing partner, but was simply Mount Hood, reminding us that we were mere mortals, tiny beings crawling around, drunk on the experience, like ants at a picnic.

Similarly, when we climbed another local volcano, Mount Rainier, Steve-o and I found ourselves pinned in our tent high on the mountain, hoping our little structure could withstand the massive windstorm that had plowed into us from the north. Those sorts of windstorms were common all over Puget Sound, the Columbia River Gorge, and into the Willamette Valley, where Portland sat. There had to be something in the code to tell me how to best build for ninety-mile-an-hour winds.

I found myself sorting through the building code like it really was a code—an ancient text written in a little-known, hardly understood ancient script. Perhaps if I could recite it into a recorder and play it backward, it would finally make sense; or if I held the book over a toaster oven, some secret message previously written in lemon juice would appear. I turned the pages and looked for diagrams; I took notes and retraced my steps through the manuals. Ultimately, I learned that it made the most sense to install a massive tension-tie in each corner, designed to withstand four thousand pounds of uplift—this is how a normal big house is made, so that's what I would do. I made little pencil drawings and scribbled the pattern for connecting bolts. Everything would be screwed and glued to prevent vibration; every facet of the building (plywood, siding, window trim, and roofing) would be clipped, stapled, and glued in all the right places. Even the placement of the screws through the plywood would be calculated—no more than six inches apart along the edges and twelve inches apart on the interior, to increase the structural stability of the plywood. This is what any carpenter would have to do if he were building a house in an earthquake zone, or in a place like the Gulf Coast where a hurricane could blow in and try to take your house apart.

The library included plenty of information for weatherizing the house too, so I planned to construct a little air gap behind the siding so the house could breathe; any rain that penetrated past the exterior cedar (driving rain created by dragging my house fifty-five miles an hour down the highway) would have a chance to evaporate inside the gap between the siding and the underlying house bits. It was an extra step in the construction, a step that would delay my ability to call the project finished, but it seemed worth the effort, especially because the front end of the house would face oncoming rain on the highway.

Of course, all this engineering led me to question why on earth I'd want to build a house on a trailer in the first place; it added such a limiting and complicating factor—a "real pain in the ass," as my father had put it—to an otherwise straightforward construction project. But I wanted my house to roll from one place to the next so I could be at home wherever I went, and I also wanted a little pointy-roofed house that looked like *home*—like Jay's cedar-clad house, like a Norman Rockwell vision of vacation, like the mountain cabins that I'd stumbled upon while backpacking. That's where I wanted to tuck myself in at night.

It wasn't all drudgery; I came to appreciate the hours at the library, smuggling coffee in under my coat and getting to know the "regulars" who slept in the big overstuffed chairs while they pretended to read. The library made me feel safe, as if every question had an answer and there was nothing to be afraid of, as long as I could sort through another volume of abstracts by the American Plywood Association. I imagined that if I read enough of these books, I could summon the courage and know-how to make a well-built house that wouldn't blast apart like a box of toothpicks when I first pulled onto the highway. I could do this. It could work!

The first step was a trailer, and after poring through the phone book and talking to men who thought I was looking for an over-the-road trailer that I could use to haul lumber, I found a metal fabricator—a welding shop—that could make a utility trailer for my house.

The shop was a smoky, dusty place just outside my neighborhood, in an area where the houses met up with pawnshops, bars, and businesses that sold used washing machines, hubcaps, and metal trailers. When I walked in, I was directed to talk to the owner, a short, swarthy Russian man. He reminded me of the teddy bear my dog had chewed—the one with the stuffing spewing out along the shoulders and neck like chest hair.

He seemed to speak very little English, so I launched into an overly loud explanation. "I need," I shouted, gesturing like I was pulling something out of the air toward my heart (the international sign for "I need"), "a trailer." For emphasis, I pancaked my hands together and pretended to drive a flat trailer (my palm) over the flat road of the other palm. The guy gave me a big smile as I made little revving sounds like a small truck. "Pratty lady," he said, laughing, flashing me his gold tooth. I missed the joke but laughed along like this was part of the discussion. I pulled a picture of Jay's house out of my pocket. "I build now," I hollered as I pointed to the photo and handed it to him.

He held the picture up to the ceiling like he was trying to see through it, and I added: "House on trailer, I make!" He suddenly looked at me with a sort of wide-eyed excitement (perhaps out of concern that I was yelling at him and using baby talk, or perhaps because he had finally realized what I wanted), and instantly I felt insecure. I crossed my arms, shifted my weight, and gave him a look like I knew precisely how deep the shit would get, like I was seasoned and savvy and had been building things my entire life. But I hadn't, and he likely knew that, so he chewed on his cigar and chuckled, and then yelled at another guy in Russian, saying something that made the other guy laugh.

A few seconds later, another younger man walked in and intervened. He was the teddy bear's son, a few years younger than me and dressed like a 1970s porn star (polyester shirt unbuttoned one too many buttons, and a pair of rayon pants that were tight on his ass and then flared to huge bell-bottoms at the ankles). He spoke something in gibberish to the other guys, and then looked at me and smiled. In broken English and with what seemed to be true sincerity, he offered, "Heelo, leedy. How can we be to heeping yours?" I instantly liked this guy, simply because I could perhaps stop yelling.

"I need a utility trailer," I explained smiling, "so I can build a house." I pointed to the picture of Jay's house, and the son nodded his head and motioned that I should follow him past the men who were now taking a break to stare at me, leaning against the wall in their baggy coveralls, smoking cigarettes and smiling.

He walked me to a parking lot in back of the building where we strolled around, looking at trailers. Over the next half hour, I was able to communicate that I didn't need sticker pockets, ramps, or tie-downs (various bits of metal that dangle off the trailer frame itself). I told him I simply needed the usual trailer "package" of metal side rails, cross braces, lights, brakes, and the ability to hold at least 3,500 pounds on each of two axles.

Through all of this, I tried to sound smart and well reasoned, but halfway through the discussion I realized I was all balled up inside, which is why I felt compelled to kick the trailer tires and knuckle-rap the metal side rails. At one point, I even kneeled down and peeked under the trailer at the metal springs strapped to the axles. "These look great," I exclaimed without knowing. I swaggered and tried to appear calm, but inside I was a mess. And all the while, the young Russian nodded his head in agreement, smiling and offering sympathetically, "You make good hoose with most kind trailer of me." It was just the confidence boost I needed, and just like that, I handed over six hundred dollars as a deposit on the trailer. "You peek her up seeks week," he said, smiling.

I walked home from the trailer place, nervously chewing my lip. Suddenly, the idea of building was real. I was all in, as they say in Vegas; I had coughed up six hundred dollars and it scared the crap out of me.

Up to that point, in my arrogance and naïveté, I'd imagined I was perfectly suited for building a house. I just needed the right how-to books and the proper tools. But walking home from the dingy trailer place, after pretending to be something I wasn't, it finally sank in that I was planning to build a house. I was going to try to build something one thousand times bigger than me, capable of rolling down the highway, never leaking, never lighting on fire, and never falling apart under the weight of all my worldly possessions. What was I thinking?

I'm certain I'd have felt less intimidated if I'd been a

carpenter instead of an office worker and inspector; my ability to locate oil drums hidden in the blackberry bushes wasn't necessarily going to help me see the subtle twist in a stick of lumber—the sort of curl that could throw everything off in the roof. But I understood there had to be something innate about building. It had to be in my genetic composition; something from my ancestors who struggled to make thatch and bog mud into a workable roof. Some part of me had to know how to build, just like you know how to blow on hot food before popping it in your mouth.

Early in life, I'd felt drawn to building, pinching little blankets to furniture and erecting forts made out of hay bales. I have a vivid memory of being about four years old and my dad wrapping his big hand around mine as we held the saw. Together we would cut boards, his body doing all the hard work, and my determination believing it was all me. Decades later, I remember doing the same thing with my niece and nephew, as we built little A-frame birdhouses for their mom.

In middle school, I drew floor plans of the tree house my dad and I would build. In high school I took woodshop, where I made my mom a lovely set of salad tongs, and in college I studied architectural engineering. I was fascinated by building, but rarely had a chance to practice the craft. It wasn't until I owned my own house that I was finally able to learn how to feed wood through a table saw, operate a nail gun, and figure out how to handle a Skilsaw.

I learned by working with real carpenters, people like my friend Katy, who seemed to know what a piece of wood was thinking. Our first project together was making kayaks—the boats that I had set up in my unfinished living room, and the project that would teach me to trust my eye when it came to hand-planing the rails and putting the finishing coat of varnish on the shell. Katy taught me how to operate a Sawzall, a pointy power tool that you hold like a machine gun and use to cut open the walls of your house when you want to install new French doors, and she showed me how to look for corkscrews in the wood that you're culling from the lumberyard.

My friend Peety taught me how to watch for rot or beetle bores when you're picking through wood at the salvage yard. He and I worked together on a plumbing project, and I ended up with a fairly fantastic crush on him because of the way he'd giggle when he was pissed; like when he got pinned in a weird position in the attic, in just such a way that he had to jam his head between the rafters right where the spiders had stowed their eggs, and then he chortled and said, "If I die from spider bites, you can have the fifty-seven cents in my pocket."

I had a first date once that involved making a kitchen countertop. We worked together as we fed wood through a table saw, with me catching the freshly cut lumber as it exited past the blade and cooing over how much fun this was (and it really was). That was the nature of my education—helpful friends and hot dates—which wasn't enough to make me a carpenter.

As I walked home from the trailer shop, I wished I were a carpenter. I wanted to walk along and shake the sawdust out of my pants cuffs, and to contemplate the pros and cons of a compound miter saw versus a simple chop saw (they look an awful lot alike). I wanted to feel confident, like my future was in good hands . . . not my own.

I was chewing my lip and staring into the small window of space directly in front of my eyes, when a movement across the street caught my attention. It was a lady and a little boy handing sheets of plywood up to a guy on the second story of a newly constructed house frame. It looked dangerous; the lady had a skirt on (a definite tripping hazard that made her look even less like a carpenter than I did), and the little boy was too short and small to do much other than keep the plywood from flipping backward. The guy above made an audible grunt as he pulled the plywood up from below.

"You want help?" I yelled.

They all turned around and looked at me, and instantly the guy said yes and his wife said, "No, we're fine."

I walked over anyway and spent the next hour lifting plywood, helping to stack it on the second floor, and leaning back to drink iced tea while I swatted the flies out of my face. They were building their own house—the three of them, but mostly the guy who reminded me a lot of my dad in his younger years: long sideburns under blond-red hair, a white T-shirt tucked into his jeans, and sweat soaking his back and chest like he'd gone swimming when we weren't looking.

"I'm building a house too," I offered. "Smaller than this but, y'know, with plywood and stuff."

And just like that, presto chango: It became real. I was going to build my house no matter what.

Anthropology 101

Now that I had my trailer on order, I needed to fully flesh out the design. I took the plans that Jay had sent me and manipulated them, switching the location of the kitchen and bathroom, the sleeping loft and living room; envisioning what it would feel like to wake up in a space the size of my back-country tent and which direction I would face while sitting in repose on the toilet. I wanted to design the house around my body and my needs, instead of following the pattern that I'd fallen into in my big house: picking paint colors and finishing the woodwork with some future owner and salability in mind. This was going to be *my* house.

I started examining the way I draped clothes over the chair in my bedroom as I undressed at night, and how I automatically reached for the light switch just below shoulder height on the right, no matter what room or building I entered. I noticed how much space I needed to chop an onion or make a peanut butter sandwich, the height of my existing kitchen counters, the cabinets and chairs. I measured the height of the toilet, the depth of my closet, and the amount of room my torso consumed when I sat up in bed. I felt like Jane Goodall, observing my behavior and wondering at the mystery of why I always brushed my teeth starting with my right bottom molars, why I always double-checked that the coffeepot was unplugged before I left for work in the morning, and why I always leaned forward with my left ear cocked when trying to define the odd sounds that I heard outside the window late at night.

The more I took note of how my body and brain clicked along through the day, the more I realized that I spent a considerable amount of time banging around with a brain full of chatter; a rush of things to do, bills to pay, telephone calls, text messages, e-mails, worrying about my job or my looks, my boobs or my ass; I rushed from thing to thing, multitasking, triple-timing, hoping to cover all the bases, avoiding anything that might disrupt the schedule or routine. At times, I was so caught up in the tempo and pattern, the predictable *tap, tap, tap* of each day, that there was no time to notice the neighbors had moved out, the wind was sneaking in from the north, the sun was shifting on its axis, and tonight the moon would look like the milky residue floating inside an enormous cereal bowl. I wondered when I had become a person who noticed so little. I had no idea that the distance from the floor to the top of my knee was twenty-four inches, which seemed to explain why I was always popping it on my car bumper.

Things had changed for me after I landed in the hospital. I truly seemed to be seeing the world in a new way, but I still needed to challenge myself to try to tune in, to notice the connections between what things were (the toilet paper holder, light switch, doorknob) and how they were connected to me, so suddenly I understood how the height of the bathtub made it easy to get in and out of the shower, and the way the handle of the front door was low enough to grasp even when my arms were full of groceries.

The overall size of my house was limited by the DOT restrictions; so it could be no taller than thirteen and a half feet from the pavement to the peak, and no wider than the wheel wells of the trailer. That meant I spent hours and days trying to sort through the pros and cons of a lower ceiling in the kitchen to accommodate a taller ceiling in the loft, and to figure out how could I cram everything I loved into a house the size of an area rug.

The bathroom and kitchen seemed to absorb the greatest amount of time, leaving me wringing my hands while I considered all the things I wanted (a small oven, three burners, pantry, refrigerator, freezer, food prep area, cupboards for dishes, drawers for tea towels, silverware, pots, pans, toaster, a shower, toilet, bathroom sink, and a place to store all my grooming tools and "boo-boo dust," as my sister and I called our lotions and potions). But there was only so much space. I made a list of the pros and cons, and argued with myself like a nutter, trying to imagine what the future me might want and what she would say about the old me's choices.

Ultimately, because of the tight quarters, I settled on imagining what would be necessary if I was staying in a remote cabin. I focused on how my friends K and Sal "glamped," as they called their form of glamorous camping when we vacationed in Hawaii. With them, it was all about the little things, so even though we each had our tents nested in the trees by the beach, complete with flying cockroaches, stinging centipedes, and an endless supply of gritty sand, we also had little grass mats outside the tents—makeshift porches where you could easily remove your flip-flops, wipe off your feet, and minimize the amount of beach that found its way into your sleeping bag. We had a tablecloth for the nearby picnic table, and at night there were candles scented like flowering plumeria and Hawaiian music to infuse the meal; and it was amazing food—Sal would take camp rations that by all rights should have tasted like salted cardboard and turn them into a gourmet affair complete with sauces and fruit slices, "candied what-cha-hoos and pickled hum-de-doos," as she named them. It was fancier living than I had most of the time at home, and that's the image I had as I argued with myself about what should or shouldn't be included in the little house.

I landed on a decision to install a small one-burner stove called the "Princess." It was a marine stove suitable for the types of meals I regularly cooked: small, elegant, and poised for something more . . . just like a princess. I had to be brutally honest with myself: I rarely used my existing four-burner stove and oven, an appliance that was labeled "Magic Chef," a mismatch for my particular flair, which was opening up soup cans and pouring the contents into a waiting pot. The Princess left room for the ceramic sink that I'd found in the crawl space of my big house, a beautiful hand-thrown bowl fitted with a tiny pipe that instead of draining to the city sewer would dribble into a giant Ball jar to be dumped in the garden. To complete my kitchen, I designed a small drop-down table that would be connected to the kitchen counter with wood hinges—clamps that would allow me to detach the table and set it on the floor on the nights that my friends and I would gather up in the tiny living room, sitting around the small table as we ate sesame noodles and listened to Getz and Gilberto jazz, and imagined nothing in the world could be more perfect than now.

At the local RV store, I tried out the various bathroom set-ups, units that allowed you to sit on the toilet while taking a shower, or to crouch in a baby bathtub with your knees near your ears while you sipped wine and enjoyed a nice tub soak. These units were almost exclusively made of fiberglass cloth impregnated with styrene (a cancer-causing chemical that smells to high heaven). Every time I did an inspection at a fiberglass shop—watching how they shot stuff out of a handheld gun, or slathered it with trowels and squeegeed out the residue, I walked away with a headache from the chemical exposure. I wanted something different in my house, and besides, the RV and travel trailer units drained to a holding tank, a big box strapped to the belly of the trailer that seemed like it'd be a pain in the neck to manage; all I'd do with my newfound free time was drive back and forth to the RV-sewage dump, repeatedly emptying the tank like my own very small bladder.

The kitchen sink would have to drain into a bucket that could be dumped in a garden, and an outdoor shower and compost toilet seemed like my only option—a sad option, for sure, as I liked the look of a small "marine head," as it was called in the boating world. The marine head is a unit, not much bigger than the butt it accommodates, which for me created a certain functional elegance. Just before I bought my big house, I'd dated a man who lived on his boat, and for our first month I never had the courage to use the toilet, in part because it was located in a tiny closet no more than a foot from where our pillows bunched together in the V-berth bed, but also because it was awkward to navigate the gentle movement of the boat while I maintained control of my stop-pee muscles for what seemed like an eternity as I ducked in, turned around, dropped my "step-ins" as we called them in childhood, backed up, and hoped for the best. It was an awkward fit, so instead I sauntered to the front of the boat, hung my tookie over the rails, and peed.

Eventually, out of need, I came to terms with the toilet and even grew to love it once I figured out the ergonomics. Sadly, the marine head required a holding tank, so a composter seemed like my only option.

I agonized over which should take up more space inside my postage stamp of a house: a refrigerator large enough to hold a week's worth of food, beer, and half-and-half, or a composting toilet that, according to the pamphlet, was too big to fit in the trunk of my car. I chose neither. I shrank the refrigerator down to the size of an undercounter icebox, and decided to adventure forward with a bucket composter—a system that required me to manage the waste along with my organic kitchen scraps in a compost barrel outside the house (a decision I made only after reading a hefty book called *The Humanure Handbook*, a really great manual that walked through the various diseases, germs, bugs, and social phobias we all carry when it comes to our poop).

The only major unknown was the shower. There wasn't any room for it inside the house; there wasn't an easy way to heat up the water, deliver it to a showerhead, and dispose of it safely. I was stuck, and after staying up till three in the morning one night, thumbing through the Lehman's catalog, which included photos of all the ways the Amish and off-grid settlers bathe, I decided to buy a membership to a gym. I figured I could get a membership at one of those big national gyms, so wherever I went from town to town, I could shower as much as I wanted. I'd heard of this happening in L.A., where hopeful would-be stars lived out of their cars with memberships to the gym. They'd sleep on the beach all day long, working on their tan, then wake up at a reasonable hour, shower at the gym, perhaps attend a casting call, then go to their bartender job till the wee hours of the morning; then back to the gym before heading home to the beach.

All of this consternation—trying to sort through how much I could bend without breaking when it came to modern conveniences—left me one part freaked out about living in the little house and one part over-the-top excited; it was like imagining what traveling to Africa to visit my friend Gina would feel like, the sound of rain on metal roofs, the smell of camel dung or food in the market, how the people would seem in Kampala versus the village where Gina was living.

It was exciting and also begged me to ask a thousand times a day: What am I doing? What is the point? And every time, something deep inside me would shoosh me and say: "Shhh, there, there. You can do this, Sweet Pea. You can build a simple, kind house . . . nothing fancy, no big deal . . . just a little house to find yourself at home."

After a month or so of playing around with layouts, after examining all of my little quirks and patterns, I came up with a floor plan for the little house. At that point, I was ready to introduce my friends to the next greatest thing, so I invited them to dinner. I greeted them at the door, masking tape in hand, and showed them the blueprint I'd taped out on the living room rug. "*This* will be the kitchen," I offered. "And this will be the bathroom," I explained, shifting my weight to the right. "The sleeping loft will be above, and *here*," I said, taking two steps forward, "is the great room." I stood on the leeward end of the rug and threw my hands over my head like pom-poms.

They stared at me with a mixture of concern and curiosity.

"Umm," one friend asked, "doesn't that make the great room [she said it with little finger quotes] the size of the dining room table?" She wanted to know if I was joking.

It wasn't a joke, but I had to admit I was curious about whether or not it could be done. I felt that it could, in the same way I was certain it would be fun to try climbing Mount Adams, Mount St. Helens, and Mount Hood all in a single weekend. Of course it was possible!

I had done this before to my friends: announced that I was going to do something even though it appeared to be out of left field. I made these dramatic proclamations, and most of the time I delivered, like the time I double-dog dared my housemate John to hang a show of his artwork at the local coffee shop. "I tell ya what, I'll do it first!" I had taunted, even though he was the real artist between us. "And you'll see how fun it is and you'll *have* to do it too." In that case, I surprised my friends (and even more so, myself) by developing enough artwork to have a little show complete with an opening-night party and by selling enough pieces to take a trip to Hawaii.

Another time, I had announced that I wanted to become an EMT because I thought it'd be awesome to "poke the siren button" in an ambulance. So I struggled through six months of training, wearing a white short-sleeved shirt with patches on the shoulders and black rayon pants that made me look like a parking attendant, and I became an EMT.

This time, I wanted to build a little house.

My friends went along with the story, and as we ate dinner sitting on the living room rug, they joked about how I could vacuum the tiny house with a tiny DustBuster and could pull it through a car wash when the windows needed cleaning. After a few beers, we played a game like Twister, tumbling over one another while standing on the rug, seeing if we could reach for a pillow off the imaginary living room couch while sitting on the toilet, or open the front door and reach for a coffee cup on the far side of the kitchen without ever stepping foot in the house. Before everyone left that night, I gave each of them something pulled randomly from the kitchen: a bottle opener, a wineglass, a ladle, or a set of pot holders that looked like chicken heads. I gave Eileen a small armada of soy sauce packages and thin wood chopsticks—leftovers from takeout— because I knew it would supplement her own perfectly matched collection. The downsizing had begun.

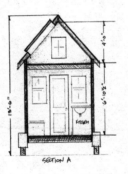

SECTION A

Dream Big,
Build Small

(MAY 2004)

Six weeks after being laughed at by the Russian welders, I got a call that my trailer was ready. Suddenly, I felt like a seven-year-old girl, standing at the far end of the high dive at the public swimming pool, my arms wrapped nervously around my chest and my wet swimsuit crawling into my butt crack, with the big kids in the water below yelling, "Go on! Do it! Jump!"

There was no more time to sit around reading books and twirling my architect ruler like a sword. At this point, I needed to believe in *me*; that my design was good enough and my skills were fair enough, and I could pick up the trailer and get cracking! I took a little warm-up lap around the living room, popped my head side to side, and shook out my legs like I used to do before a race. It was time to get started.

I borrowed a truck from my friend Barb, who had borrowed it from another friend, and together we drove over to the trailer place, giggling with excitement. I raced into the office feeling like an expectant adoptive mother and settled up the bill in what must have been record time. I was sweating so intensely I could feel the salt landing in my bra, and a moment later spilling down my stomach into my jeans, and then finally we marched out to the back parking lot. My jaw dropped. The trailer was perfect, with shiny black side rails, heavy-duty axles, deeply treaded tires, and taillights that seemed to twinkle and spit cute bubbles out of their mouths as we walked up.

I don't remember saying anything other than a strong "Got it" as the foreman showed us how to connect the lights and brakes and explained in broken English that the cross-hitch chains were critical. "They are for keep trailer," he said, pointing at the trailer hitch, "from go to bye-bye." He offered this last part as he pantomimed me supposedly waving good-bye to my house and the trailer as I drove up a hill.

"Got it." I smiled. Over the next ten minutes, I proceeded to spit out the same thing another fifteen or sixteen times, saying it with a nod, like a genius, like I had grown up around trailers and had studied metal fabrication at university; but in reality, I was so excited it was impossible to track all the information. All I could hear was the rabble in my head saying "Wow, wow, wow-wow-wow!" as we walked around the trailer, and all I could say in the end was "Lug nuts, got it."

The library books never said anything about checking the lug nuts every so often, or minding the cross-hitch chains to avoid a runaway load. I summoned my courage and looked at my friend as we pulled into traffic, both of us grinning nervously and leaning forward into the dashboard. We arrived at my house twenty minutes later, after motoring along slower than five miles an hour, waving other vehicles around us, and collectively screaming "Whoa!" as we went over a tiny neighborhood speed bump. I turned off the ignition with a big "Woo hoo!" and then noticed that I was four feet from the curb, still sitting in the street. "Whatever," I told Barb, "let's go get a cup of coffee to celebrate!"

I positively swaggered with adrenaline as we walked around the corner to the coffee shop. Barb and I spied a neighbor who lived down the street, and he gave us a nod and said, "Saw your trailer a minute ago. Sweet!" He was a building contractor, a short, stocky guy with a thick neck, and the sort of man who in the dark might be mistaken for a badger. By his comment, I immediately felt that I'd been accepted into a special club where everyone wore flannel, was successful in a shovel-in-hand sort of way, and often said things like "Hold my beer" before doing something powerfully dangerous.

"I hope to start building tomorrow," I said, holding my crossed fingers up in the air and looking skyward like I was praying for rain, and instantly feeling that this gesture placed me well outside the flannel shirt crowd.

He nodded. "Nice. Can that trailer fit up the driveway? The city won't let you keep it on the street . . . fascists." He said this shaking his head, like a piece of gravel could fall out, and if it did, he would have given it to me to throw at City Hall.

"Ya. Right. I know," I said firmly, while inside I screamed, *Shit, shit, shit-shit-shit!*

There was no way I could back the trailer up the steep rampart that defined the front of my driveway. And even if I could drag it up and over the steep slope, the drive was so narrow it would be impossible to pull ladders alongside. There was barely room to open a car door, let alone set a ladder and maneuver plywood up over your head to the roof. I needed another solution, and in the meantime maybe it could just sit on the curb, looking cute.

Later in the day, I mentioned the driveway conundrum to my friend Camelli, who lived across the street. She was an engineer for the city, so I figured she'd know the inside scoop and would set me straight. We'd met years ago, in college, when she was a freckle-faced freshman with the driest sense of humor on the planet; she would play wry jokes on her housemates, as when one of them was grilling a chicken and she stole it from the grill while he wasn't looking. When he returned and found it missing, he thought he was crazy, and he headed for the kitchen, scratching his head, at which point she returned the chicken to the grill. She repeated this process twice, each time returning to her spot in the living room, where, when her housemate stormed past looking for his lost chicken, she'd tuck her hair behind her ears and adjust her glasses, flipping a page in her book like she'd been studying the whole time. "What do you think the city would do if I parked the trailer on the curb for a month?" I asked her. "Fine me? Tow me?"

After a bit of thought, she invited me to build in her drive-way, explaining that she wasn't using it or her garage. In retro-spect, I wonder if she knew what I didn't: There was no earthly way that I could build a house in a month, working alone and only on weekends. It would take at least three months, and in that time, working in the street would not only be illegal, it'd be dangerous. Leave it to Camelli to be logical and generous.

The trailer fit perfectly in her driveway, and I spent the next hour measuring everything: the trailer's width and length, the depth of the side rails and wheel wells, the height from the pavement up to the top of the trailer, the distance between ribs, the size of the tires, the location of the lights, and the distance diagonally from the front of the trailer to the back corners. I used this information to redraw my plans for the floor frame and walls, and then I pulled together a list of every stick of wood I'd need to start things out.

The list looked small and suddenly beautiful, like I was

studying a list of pieces that I hoped would grow from my wishful thinking into something called "floors," "walls," "roof,"
"little house," and "home."

"Here we go," I whispered to RooDee. "We're gonna build
a house."

The next day, I ventured off to the lumberyard with my
Post-it note in one hand and a tape measure in the other. I
started by culling through a giant pile of "studs" (a word that
totally made sense given the fact that these were the strong
pieces of wood that would hold up the roof, define the walls,
and keep my little house in shape), pulling sticks of wood from
the pile and searching each one for the slightest hint of a twist
or warp, just like Katy had taught me. Almost immediately,
while lifting one stick of wood off the other, I slammed a sliver
into the palm of my hand, causing me to twirl around in pain,
clutching my hand like I'd rammed it into a wood chipper. I
stood in the center of the aisle, staring and probing at the meat
on my hand, and then chewed the sliver out, biting it because
my fingers couldn't do the job—an act that made me feel clever
and brave.

I was thinking on my feet. Injury number one: no big deal.

Over the next half hour, three different men offered to help
me, making me wonder if someone had made a secret an-
nouncement about a skinny blonde who was sucking her fist in
the lumber department. I was too proud to accept their help,
offering a quick "Oh, that's sweet, but I've got it" as I continued

to sort through the wood alone, gingerly picking up each stick like it could be tethered to an electric prod.

I loaded the wood on a small pushcart, with two twelve-foot sticks balanced in the center and poking out in front like a lance. The cart weighed a ton and I had to really put my weight into it to roll it toward the cash register. Seconds into the haul, I realized things weren't going well. I was headed for a display rack, so I grabbed the back of the cart, but too late. The lumber slammed into the rack, knocking it over and ramming the lance backward into my pelvis, doubling me up like I'd swallowed a tire iron.

Injury number two that day was a sadly placed goose egg, which paled compared to injury number three: my pride.

Things had gotten off to a bumpy start, but soon enough I was working my way through a stack of lumber, building the floor frame, and then attaching aluminum sheathing to create an undercarriage. I felt like a woman learning to swim, awkwardly paddling over to my drill and then slowly treading water as I tried to get my bearing around a piece of wood; daring myself to dunk my head underwater as I measured, then remeasured, and finally cut the floor joists to length. It was exhausting and exhilarating.

During the workweek, I entertained my coworkers with stories about sunburning the inside of my mouth as I panted, openmouthed, over the aluminum undercarriage, struggling to fit it in place; and oddly, I found myself calmer than I'd been in a long while. Maybe it was simply because my muscles ached or maybe because I felt that nothing was more compelling than the stack of wood that was waiting in Camelli's garage, but whatever the reason, I was relaxed as I discussed problems with a factory worker, and less overwhelmed when I realized there was nothing I could do about the way "acceptable levels" of radioactive mud were being deposited in a pond at the edge of town.

After my second or third weekend of consecutive twelve-hour days, I realized that I might have underestimated how long it would take to finish the house. I had the floor framed, complete with metal undercarriage, rigid foam insulation, and plywood deck; and I also had the walls framed out and resting on the ground nearby. But that was it . . . hardly a house. At the rate I was going, it would take me no less than a year to have a livable structure, and by then my back, arms, legs, fingers, and earlobes would be reduced to nubbins. Every part of my body ached: my scalp from walking with plywood balanced on my head, my feet from dropping wood, tools, boxes, and bins on my unprotected flip-flopped feet (the reason real carpenters wear steel-toed boots). My shins, elbows, armpits, the webs between my fingers, my cheekbones, knuckles, hip sockets, and the tiny hairs above my kneecaps—everything hurt, but I kept at it, and finally the floor was in place and the walls were prefabricated, sitting in a neat stack near the trailer. Now it was time to wrangle my friends to help me lift the walls into place, square them up, and secure them to the trailer.

I called as many friends as possible, luring them with beer, pizza, and the idea of a good old-fashioned barn raising, right in the heart of the city. "It'll be more fun than an Amish rake fight," I'd promised, and sure enough, my friends arrived, carting their tools, food, pets, and children. I remember looking around at one point, and someone had pulled a red wagon full of beer over to the house, food was sitting on a table made out of the tailgate of someone's nearby truck, dogs was lounging under the trailer, and a couple of my friends' kids were having a sword fight with long, skinny balloons, chasing each other around a picnic blanket that had been thrown on the ground in the nearby yard. I was so happy standing there, seeing what was happening around my house.

In a single day, my friends and I stabilized the trailer, jacking it up onto cinder blocks to level it, and then we hoisted the walls into place on the platform. Now, where there had previously been an odd-looking trailer and a few piles of wood, there was something that was starting to look like . . . well, like something. It all went faster than I thought it would—a million times faster than if I'd been working alone, instantly going from a two-dimensional drawing to a colossal enclosure. I stood on the platform and pointed to a couple of two-by-fours on the wall and stuck my head through like I was taking in the fresh air on a spring day. "Check out my perfect view of the night sky," I called. My friends stood on the ground two feet below me, and miles away from understanding why I would want to sleep on a trailer platform. They gazed at me with big smiles and unfixed eyes, their eyebrows raised expectantly; things got quiet with a giant pregnant pause settling between us, and then Steve-o (my trusty climbing partner and a former housemate) screamed out of the blue, with a massive smile on his face and his eyes trained on me, fists pumping wildly in the air: "Deeeeee Willllllliams!!!" like I'd just head-chipped a soccer ball into the goal with two seconds left in the game.

I loved Steve-o more than ever for that. I couldn't possibly begin to explain what was only beginning to bud inside me: I wanted a home. I wanted to *be* at home, in the world and in my body (a feeling I had been missing since I'd woken up in the hospital) and somehow, in some as yet undefined way, I knew that windows in the great room and a skylight over my bed were going to help with that.

Over the next several weeks, I discovered a nice rhythm for lifting, schlepping, drilling, cutting, fitting, refitting, and re-refitting. It wasn't a perfect process; I was learning as I went. For example, one day, I spent an entire morning putting up rafters. After screwing in each and every one, squeezing between them and balancing on the skeleton of the house, I took a break and went for coffee around the corner. On my way back, I finally had a chance to see the roof for the first time. Along the peak, every rafter had been screwed left of center, resulting in a shift to the left that made my roof look like a Nordic ship, lunging forward like an Olympic diver headed over the bow into the water. I stood there staring, trying not to cry, and then I crawled back on the roof to redrill, rescrew, and reset the roof.

When I got stuck with something, like trying to trim out a window, I'd collect RooDee from her hiding spot under Camelli's rhododendrons, and we'd go for a walk through the neighborhood, examining various window sashes, rafter tails, roofing details, skylight flashing, the size and spacing of siding, and the way pointy roofs have a piece of wood on the eave so a gutter can be hooked on.

At night, after I'd tuck into bed, I'd pull from a stack of books one telling me how to wire the electric lights and install metal plates on the studs so I wouldn't pound a nail into the electric wires. I'd flip through the pages while my dog snored nearby, while my housemates made popcorn and watched a movie downstairs, and while the rest of the world whizzed by at a billion miles an hour.

During lunch at work, I'd read about how to seal up the siding and tuck tar paper around the doorjamb to keep it from leaking; I'd learn about gable roofs, overhangs, and the best way to install cedar siding. At dinner, I'd read about alternative insulation, advanced wall framing, and how to install corrugated metal roofing; I'd read pamphlets with glossy photos of cork flooring, bamboo wallboard, and environmentally friendly paints available at the local eco-building store. And all the while, I'd put my faith in these books, hoping they would set me straight and show me how to keep from sparking my shoes on fire while using a circular saw to cut into the metal roofing.

Book learning was always big in my family, with both my mom and dad having gone to graduate school and slogging through doctoral programs. All my siblings went to college, and we all called ourselves "middle class," which doesn't really mean anything to me anymore. Does it mean you're a blue-collar worker like my nephew, who went into the Air Force right out of high school and now operates dirt-moving equipment with tires bigger than my car, or a bureaucrat (like me) who went to graduate school but makes less money than her nephew? Does being middle class mean you can relax, that you've arrived because you bought a house you can barely afford, but no matter, because you are now a part of what some people call the "owning class"? In any case, whatever you call me, my parents encouraged me to go to college and become a book lover, and to trust that I could do nearly anything if I could find the right book at the library.

It was true; books had saved me in my home remodeling projects, but they fell short in teaching me how to trust my instincts, and how to stop thinking with my educated brain and more with my kneecaps and butt cheeks. There was no book that could teach me how to use my spine, quads, and lats to squat-thrust and pick up a stack of wood that weighed nearly as much as me. Most of my building education came in the form of my right hand learning how to best hold the drill while my left hand was discovering how to simultaneously grip a piece of wood and maintain the proper angle for driving a screw through it.

When I was close to being done with the house, someone asked me what the hardest part had been, and I found myself staring at my feet, wishing they could speak for me, since they likely knew more than me after taking so much abuse. I looked at my arms, the torn skin and scrapes, and I wondered what my wrist muscles would remember long into the future.

And then I thought about the day I glued my hair to the house. It was early on in the project and I was working alone. I was using my head to hold a piece of plywood true as I screwed it to the wall, a technique that had been relatively effective so far. But this time, part of my ponytail got stuck behind the plywood and glued into the skin of my house. I stood there, trapped and twisted at an angle, imagining that I might have to slowly chew through my hair to free myself. I ended up screaming at Camelli to come help, hoping she was home and that she'd hear me. All the while, my hands were looking for a solution, scanning with their fingertips, palms, and pads to understand my hair-pinned predicament. Now that I think of it, maybe my hands were secretly in on that practical joke, tired of the way my hair was always swooshing around like a Barbie doll's, tired of constantly attending to the hair . . . putting it up in a ponytail, pulling it out of my eyes, picking sawdust out of it at the end of the day. My hands probably secretly disliked the neediness of my hair; they were the real workhorses of the project. They were the real power tools that had stepped up (so to speak) and thrown themselves into service, and it looked like it. Even though I was only a few weeks into building, I had developed what my friends and I called "man hands": scarred, knobby, muscled hands with square palms like slices of bread. They were working hands. Strong hands. "Man hands" stuck, in my case, to a lady's arms. Recently, when I got together with my father, we both casually reached for the same cup of coffee, both of us extending the same blackened fingernail toward the mug. I'd smashed mine under a load of lumber, and he'd smashed his trying to fix his lawn mower.

Maybe my hands didn't care about my hair because, in re-ality, they were just my hands—my powerful man hands doing man things, getting stuff done, operating power tools, driving the car, using a hammer one minute, doing something delicate the next, like feather-dusting fingertips along a freshly sanded piece of wood as if they were stroking the soft peach earlobes of a baby.

As it turned out, Camelli was home and could hear me; she came out and saw what had happened, raised one finger and smiled, disappeared, and a minute later returned with a camera.

While she snapped photos, I screamed about my hair and how my head was turned at a bad angle, and "I might have

cranial fluid draining out my ear soon." I spit out this information while giggling so hard I thought I'd pee. "Holy shit,
Camelli," I screamed and cackled, "this is serious!" Camelli
looked at me and again said nothing, but disappeared once
more into her house. She returned a minute later, smiling, with
a pair of scissors to release me.

We both laughed and laughed and laughed, and later that
night, as I assessed my new lopsided haircut, I cried. I had
been working to grow out my hair for a long time. I say "working" because I really wanted long hair—the sort of hair that
would blow back in a giant fireball of sexiness—but so far I
hadn't had the patience to get there; instead I'd respond to a
certain siren call where I'd get annoyed by my bangs flopping
in my eyes and bothered by how I couldn't puff them out of the
way. It was exhausting work, puffing away at my bangs, so typically at some frustrated moment, I'd grab a pair of scissors to
trim my bangs, then the sides, then the bangs again, and then
the sides, till all that was left was someone who looked like
Friar Tuck of yon forest.

Somehow, distracted by months of reading, planning, and
building, I had survived those critical junctures that previously
led me to the scissors, leaving me with locks that landed mid-
spine. So, late that night, after lopping off three inches of hard-
won hair, I cried. I stared in the mirror, and then suddenly out
of my blubbering, I started to laugh.

After that, I worked with a zip knife in my pocket.

//////////////

As I continued to shop for wood and parts, I probably made things harder for myself than they needed to be by trying to pin down the story behind the materials I was using. Ever since I'd gotten out of the hospital, I felt that everything had a story. I knew some of that story because I'd done inspections at mills and factories—at the places that make cold-rolled steel into snap-lock roofing, and fir into preserved wood that was cooked in a concoction of copper, arsenic, and chromic acid. But there were volumes that I still didn't know. I remember standing in front of a salesclerk at the lumberyard, asking where their lumber came from, what forest and who logged it, and what mill turned it into the two-by-fours and plywood that I was about to purchase. She looked at me like I had a fake axe sticking out my head; momentarily horrified and then simply annoyed. She didn't know, didn't want to find out, and I ended up buying the wood anyway, hoping that I was making a good choice.

As often as possible, I shopped at a local place called Mr. Plywood. It was in my neighborhood, the guys there loaded the wood on my car for me, and they chuckled when I asked them to come home with me to unload it. (I really did just want them to unload it. I fantasized about them saving my sore muscles by unloading the whole lot, and instead of helping, I'd just smile, say thanks, and hand each of them a cold beer.) I also shopped at the local hardware store, buying drill bits and tools, sandpaper and saw blades while shooting the breeze with the grandpa-owner and his grandson—choosing their goods even though the prices were higher than they were at the nearby retail chain store.

Also in the interest of doing the right thing, I tried to use up every bit of wood, probably spending as much time slowly pawing through the scrap pile as I did actually building the house. I meant well; I knew the landfills were chock-full of construction debris—something I'd learned by sorting through dumpsters at construction sites, and also from work. A few months before I started working on my little house, I had investigated why birds were dropping dead in the fly zone that existed inches above a landfill's surface, a problem that was eventually attributed to ten thousand tons of chicken feathers, beaks, and feet (courtesy of the local meatpacking plant) that were decaying along with acres of construction debris. Somehow the chemistry and placement of those wastes had generated a poisonous concentration of hydrogen sulfide, a rotten-egg gas so toxic that anything flying over dropped dead.

Besides my obsessive, possibly neurotic focus on minimizing my trash, I also found myself completely infatuated with second-use materials: old floorboards, sinks, light fixtures, and windows. I swooned as I stood on the curb, looking at a pile of building debris, or while I palmed my way through a box of old faucets at the salvage yard. I'm not sure why I loved the old stuff so much. It seemed heavier—weighted down with lead instead of aluminum, and layered with time. It was beautiful to me and I'd imbue it with some sort of past life; a bit of fiction that I'd make up when, for example, I'd find an old doorknob, worn down to expose the copper plating beneath the bronze finish, and suddenly I'd imagine that some old couple had turned that knob day in and day out for fifty years, coming and going to work, the grocery store, their kids' piano recitals, and later (much later) their kids' weddings. That knob was the first thing they'd touched after their trip to Paris, a trip they'd planned for decades, saving money and trying to find time between grandkids and a hip replacement and a big scare with cancer. The music that wafted along the Champs-Élysées and the click of the front doorknob, followed a second later by "Sweetheart, I'm home," would be playing at the back of each of their minds as they drifted into sleep and then later into death.

Years later, the door (knob and all) was replaced in a big home remodel, and luckily the unit would find its way to the salvage yard and into the hands of little ladies like me looking for a bit of sweet history.

I liked building my house out of materials that could tell a good story, like this: The whole front of my house is sheathed in old-growth cedar, trees that were likely at least five hundred years old when they were cut down in the 1940s, milled into long tight-grained beveled boards, and sold to a guy who lived in Portland, Oregon. After he got them and sheathed his own house, he stored the leftovers in the attic of his garage, where they sat until the summer of 2004, when I was building my little house.

He walked over one day as I was finishing the roof of my house, and cooed over the way I'd doubled up the metal sheeting near the ridge so it offered a nice weighty cap. I didn't have the courage to tell him that I'd measured wrong when installing the roofing and had to tack a short piece near the ridge like a toupee.

I had known this guy for years; he lived a few houses down from me, and we hardly ever exchanged words other than "Hello" and "How ya doing." He always walked by with his small pug-faced dog in one arm and a short piece of metal pipe in the other hand "to beat back any big dog that tries to take a bite out of Henry here," he'd explained while nodding at his mutt. He struck me as a gruff, quietly mean old guy, but there he was, standing below me with his pipe and dog, admiring my roof.

"Think you could come see what's wrong with my garage roof?" he asked, and I obliged, walking down the street in my flip-flops, and wondering at this new, kind guy—my new best friend. He explained along the way that the roof had started sagging in one spot, and he wanted to know how to best fix it.

I crawled up a ladder into the garage attic, and that's when I noticed the old cedar siding stacked up to the rafters, covered in dust. I squirmed past the bundle, balancing on the collar ties that made up a makeshift floor, and was able to diagnose his roof problem: "You got a busted rafter up here, but we could likely jack it back into place and sister another rafter alongside." I said all of this with a bit of swagger, like a member of the Flannel Shirt Club.

"Humm," he huffed as he squinted up through the dust floating in the sunlight between me and him.

"And," I continued, "you've got a lot of wood up here that might be putting some stress on the old girl, so you might want to think about moving it."

"Oh, that's the stuff I got when Cathy and I first built this place, back when your house and mine were nearly the only ones on this block. Back when there was a milking barn where the music store sits," he muttered.

"Humm," I offered.

"Maybe you could move it down here? Maybe use it on your little shed?"

"Well . . . I guess so," I offered, while inside screaming *Jackpot!* and dreaming about how it would feel to have five-hundred-year-old trees—beautiful trees, Oregon trees—wrapped around my house. I'd have preferred to stand in the living forest that begat that stack of lumber—the way a big forest like that filters the light, and everything smells damp and earthy, and it seems like every molecule is breathing—but that wasn't up to me, so I'd be grateful to settle for the next-best thing: the most stunning beveled siding I'd ever seen.

"You fix that rafter and it's all yours."

I hopped down the ladder and raced home for a car jack and some wood to repair his roof, cackling, "Pinch my ass, I'm dreaming!" I never saw this coming—the little house was working its magic, connecting me to people and materials I never would have guessed would find their way into the picture.

I had to spend a lot of time remilling the old cedar so it would match up with the new wood from the lumberyard, and like a total nutball, I spent an entire precious day resawing the thin (two-inch-wide) cedar that I'd ripped off the siding so I could make it into usable window trim. It worked, and years into the future, I still love sitting in my living room, looking up at the skylight and seeing the kerf marks on the old cedar that outlines the window.

Blondie on the Roof

I spent all of June and half of July mostly working alone, never taking a weekend off, jumping out of my car the minute I got home from work during the week. Over time, my little house and the "blondie on the roof," as one passerby described me, became something of a neighborhood spectacle. One day, a complete stranger stopped as he was driving by because he saw me carrying one of the skylight windows up to the roof. He parked his car, threw an extra ladder up next to me, and started working, explaining that he was on his way to see his mom, who lived in the retirement home down the street. "She'd give me an earful if I told her I saw you crawling up a ladder in flip-flops and I did nothing to save you from killing yourself." It was a comment that could have seemed condescending, but this kind man was serious, and he was helpful.

I've never been good with asking for help; it seems risky, but at some point when things are really dicey, your stubbornness gives way to a certain form of humility that, after you get over yourself, feels liberating. I started to believe that the universe was conspiring to help me finish my house, sending people along at the right moment. I never learned that man's name, but I was certain he happened along at a time that saved my life or the life of the skylight that now sits over the great room. Either way . . . he did his mother right. Halfway up the ladder, my defibrillator had started firing, causing me to suddenly lean my head into the window glass and clutch the entire unit with the ladder in a bear hug. I was frozen, waiting for the storm to pass, and when I saw that second ladder slam against the roof next to me, I knew that whatever happened next, it was going to be all right. I was safe.

Sometimes the word *gratitude* feels too thin to explain things, and I started to cry, then almost immediately giggle like a ten-year-old, when we finally got the window in place.

Another time, a traveling salesman (a twenty-year-old college student selling magazine subscriptions off his bike) rode over and collapsed his wares on the nearby lawn. We chitchatted, with me on the roof and him lying back on the grass, sipping water; we discussed the little house, how it was built, and what I planned to do with it. "Are you gonna live in it?" he asked, leaning up on his elbows. I stopped what I was doing and pulled my sunglasses up on my head, looking across the street at my big beautiful house. The chocolate mint was blooming near the lavender, and the small apple tree in the front yard was positively beaming with its first baby fruit—a green apple the size of a chicken egg. The fir tree was shadowing the left side of the house, and the sun was glinting off the window on the right, making the house look like it was winking at me.

"I'm selling my big house over there"—I nodded across the street—"and building this."

"Oh," he said, glancing over at the house; it seemed to look to both of us like the best place in the world to take a nap. "That's cool," he offered, and then went on to tell me about always wanting to live in a beach cabin, where you'd cook up whatever fish you caught during the day, when you weren't surfing and, "y'know, having fun," and at night you'd sleep listening to the waves roll in.

"That sounds sweet," I offered with a quick smile and a deep breath. "Hey, I gotta make a little noise here. Soak up the sun for me." And with that I went back to my drill and impact driver, installing the metal roofing and chewing my lip as I went because I had just admitted for the first time that I was going to sell my house.

There was a part of me that must have thought I'd get tired halfway through the building; I'd blow myself out, pull up short, and call it quits, and then I'd go back to life as usual. But that hadn't happened. I had worked my way through a thousand problems, like when the tar paper bulged on the corners so I used a strap wrapped around the whole house and ratcheted it tight to attach the trim; I had figured that out without using a book, and that was just one of a bunch of ideas that had saved the day. I liked it; I was falling in love with the way my knees knew how to hold a piece of plywood halfway up till I could grab the underside with my hand. I liked the way the little house was taking shape, and the way it seemed to double-dog dare me to step in . . . *move* in.

I had been thinking about it for weeks, and had even sent a few "feelers" to friends in Olympia, propositioning them by saying, "Wouldn't it be funny if I finished my house and then moved into your backyard, ha-ha?" And just now, talking about it with the salesman, I realized that was just what I wanted. Maybe.

A week later, I took the weekend off to attend the wedding of John, my old housemate. John and I had lived together for three years as he worked his way through college and then into a doctoral program, and then he was off to the races once he fell in love with Brenda. They had lived in Washington, D.C., for a short while, then came back to Seattle, and now they were getting hitched.

I arrived at the rehearsal dinner wearing flip-flops, a sunburn, and a Hawaiian dress, feeling a little like someone who had just been rescued off a desert island and couldn't remember how to sip water out of anything but a coconut husk. I remember laughing with John and Brenda, their parents, and other friends, but all the while I was thinking about the little house at home. I behaved like a new mother, showing off photos of my half-finished house and entertaining friends with stories about the way I'd glued my hair to the house and nearly shot myself off a ladder using a drill to fight off a bee.

"Shut the front door!" John had laughed, using the nearly naughty F-word phrase we had often spit out when we were amazed by something. "I love that," he cackled as I blathered on about my adventure.

Later that night, I settled into a sailboat that Brenda's folks had loaned me so RooDee and I would have a place to sleep. The marina was beautiful with the moon reflected over the water and the halyards gently chiming off the masts, and the boat was ideal for holding me in my quandary. Sitting there in a space not much bigger than the shower stall at home, I made a list of pros and cons for selling my house. On the plus side, I could live debt free and in a house that would take ten seconds to clean. On the minus side, I would be giving up everything I'd worked so hard to achieve: a nice house and beautiful gardens, a sense of placement and home.

"Home . . ." I muttered out loud as I looked at my dog snoring next to me, paws occasionally flipping as she dreamed of running across an open meadow, chasing woodchucks. "And what is that but the place that when you go there, they have to take you in?" I offered this last part as I rubbed RooDee's belly, remembering Robert Frost's poem about the hired man who returned to the place he felt most comfortable, just before he passed away. The question had been asked in a poem eighty years ago, and again now as I listened to seagulls muttering about dinner. What was the next-best place for RooDee and me?

I loved my house, but more and more I felt I didn't belong there. It was the place where I slept. In the mornings, I'd spend just enough time there to take a shower, realize my clothes were still in the dryer, and race downstairs naked for fresh undies, a shirt, and pants before jaunting off to work. The rest of my waking hours I spent across the street, working on the little house. And my house was increasingly empty. My housemates Holly and Sam had moved out, dragging what they could in their suitcases to Hawaii; and my housemate Lisa spent more of her time at her boyfriend David's house.

There was something missing for me, but I couldn't quite put my finger on it. More and more, while standing in the living room, I felt like someone who'd just had a tooth pulled and was searching the open hole repeatedly with her tongue. I mentioned the idea of selling the house to a few friends, and mostly heard some version of "Why would you do that? It just started looking good." And that was true. I had turned myself inside out working on the house, and had come to love it; at least, I supposed I loved it. Maybe it wasn't love so much as a fear of losing everything I'd accomplished. I was afraid to let go.

Years ago, I'd gone skydiving with my friend Bryan. After

ten hours of training, we were loaded like eggs into a cardboard carton—I describe it this way because there were no seats, no seat belts or overhead compartments, no oxygen masks that would drop out of the ceiling should the cabin experience a sudden drop in pressure; instead there was the thin plane casing wrapped around us like we were sitting in a metal colon, ready for expulsion. The twin-engine plane was so old and rickety that it seemed it would be a relief to fend for ourselves outside, even if "outside" was three thousand feet up. Bryan jumped first, waving at me and smiling as he flew past the tiny window where I was crouched at the back of the plane. After a few more people jumped, it was my turn. I worked my way out onto the wing strut, moving hand over hand, just like we'd been trained. I hung there gripping the aluminum wing, my feet dangling in space with the earth spinning slowly below me, leaving me imagining what my fellow humans were doing down there. I couldn't even see them. Their cars, along with mine, stationed in the airport parking lot, looked like the aphids that regularly attacked my garden greens. Suddenly, I felt that I could suspend myself there for centuries; there was no way I was letting go of the fucking plane. I looked over at the jumpmaster who had taught the class and who was now sitting in the door of the plane shouting at me to "LET GO!" I shook my head back and forth, and stared straight ahead at the horizon. I felt calm and clearheaded. A few minutes later, I heard a clunking sound near my head. I looked back at the door. The jumpmaster was holding a short stick, a sawed-off broom handle that he was banging on the wing a few inches from my fingers.

"LET GO!" he yelled again, and then slammed the stick on the wing.

I knew what he meant. He had kidded with us that if we didn't let go at the proper moment, he would slap our hands with the stick, and we had all laughed because who would be silly enough to hang on when they should let go?

Finally, after a few minutes, I summoned the courage to let go. I arched my back, arms above my head like a cheerleader, and then watched as the plane turned into a tiny toy floating above me. The free fall was as exhilarating as it was terrifying, and once my parachute was deployed, the rest of the ride was beautiful, giving me a chance to see Puget Sound and Mount Olympus, and the multitude of forest, farms, and bogs that separated the two. It was like seeing your head finally connected to your feet for the first and only time. In that case, letting go was a blessing . . . everything turned out just fine.

In record time, with hardly any hard work—no hand wringing or paintbrush dabbing that normally goes with the territory—I sold the house to my friend Kimo. In a matter of a few days, we figured out the paperwork and arranged for her to move in—lock, stock, and barrel—on Labor Day weekend, about a month away, when I would load my truck and tow my little house and new life up to Olympia.

Boom. Just like that.

Right when I'd hatched this newer, more interesting plan for my little house (no longer a simple project but a soon-to-be home), my folks came to visit. They came to see me, my grandma, and other nearby family members as part of an elaborate plan where they'd also trailer a boat from the West Coast, where it was purchased, back to the Midwest where they lived. They had arrived the day before, Dad's dream boat in tow, and had marveled at the progress I'd made on the little house; the roof was half done and looking spectacularly shiny, and the shell was sheathed in tar paper ready to receive the cedar siding. I walked them around, showing them the salvaged goods that I'd collected: the neighbor's siding, the old door, the cedar floorboards, and a giant brass porthole that I planned to install in the aft gable wall. They were fantastically enthused, oohing and aahing at all the right moments.

And then it was time to get back to work. I thought I'd enlist my mom to help me pick up a load of cedar siding. We erected scaffolding on top of my tiny car, lashing an extension ladder to the roof rack and tying a red ribbon on the end for safety's sake. Then we were off. The idea was to lay the extra-long cedar siding on top of the extension ladder to support it and keep it from sliding off my extra-short car. It was a brilliant idea, but a few minutes into the trip (and now on the highway), I realized that my mother and I were likely sustaining significant hearing loss due to the roar of wind whipping past the ladder rungs. We weren't bonding very well either, as we shouted over the roar and she tried to catch me up on the family gossip.

It went like this:

"SHE SAID, 'GO TO HELL'?" I shouted at my mom, alarmed and wondering why my niece would say that to my dad.

"NO!" my mom yelled back. "SHE SAID, 'GOING WELL.'" She looked at me like I was trying to start trouble.

I paused and frowned. "YOU'RE NOT GOING TO TELL?" This was such a weird conversation. What the hell was happening in my family?

And so it went for an hour.

My mom and I arrived home to find my dad and brother trying to shove my old queen-size futon mattress into the cockpit of the sailboat. I had offered my brother the futon, the couch frame that it rested on, some rugs, and anything else he wanted to take home, since I obviously wasn't going to need this stuff in my new tiny house.

It was a fantastic idea except for the fact that the mattress kept getting hung up on the boat rigging and the guys were having a hard time squeezing the fluff past the extra-small galley door. My dad and brother were sweating and swearing, and my mom quickly hopped out of the car, looking relieved to be standing on firm ground. I started snickering, but quickly realized this was serious business.

"Just grab the damn edge!" my dad spat at my brother.

"There is no 'edge,'" my brother shot back. "Fracking fracker!" He then punched the futon with his forehead.

When they finally shoved it through the door, my brother slapped it and cheekily said he was sure it would be easier to remove than it was to install. "It'll be like delivering a baby . . . now how hard can that be?" He chuckled as my dad rolled his eyes.

Later that night, we all sat on the front porch and stared across the street at my half-finished little house. It was a sorrowful sight—a tarpaper shack, chocked up on cinder blocks. Neighbors and friends had used white chalk to graffiti the sides, drawing funny faces and slogans like "Eat Here" and "Get Gas." I couldn't decide which reminded me more of *The Grapes of Wrath*: my little cabin or my dad's boat, which now leaned with the weight of furniture as knickknacks cluttered the bow. Sipping our beers, we were both held captive and silent, dreaming of what was next—to the sea or the shallows, alone or with others.

They left a few days later, dragging a boatload of household items with them; leaving me with a living room that echoed and a better understanding of my family wiring. It was wacky and illogical to trailer a twenty-five-foot sailboat for eighteen hundred miles, and it made no sense to anyone but my dad, but he didn't care. He didn't ask for anyone's permission or approval. And a week later, while my mom clutched the guard rails, my dad launched his boat at a local Missouri reservoir,

amid drowned-out scrub oak and above former rolling grass-
lands, happy as a clam as he sailed from one side of the tiny
lake to the other.

That obstinate sense of independence was the biggest challenge I faced in building my little house (that, and not always
knowing what I was doing). I was stubborn in the way I hated
to ask for help. Some people are good at it, asking friends or
their husband to collect ginger ale and crackers at the grocery
because they feel nauseous, or standing on the side of the road
with a tire iron in one hand, hoping someone will stop to change
their flat tire. I'm not like that; I'd rather have a rough stick
dragged across my gums than walk to the neighbor's house to
borrow sugar or ask for help jump-starting my car.

In the first few weeks that I was building, I'd loaded and
unloaded all the lumber myself, hefting sheets of plywood that
weighed sixty pounds—more than half my own weight—up
onto the roof rack of my car and then off it and into the garage.
I had sorted through the framing, figuring out how to build the
undercarriage and floor bracing. I went into work every morning
with my new man hands, with knuckle scrapes, splinters, finger
cuts, and sore muscles, but I have to admit: I liked it. It felt
good to be working and building new muscles. I remember falling asleep one night doing a little inventory: my ear was swollen from nearly ripping it off while moving plywood (I had a
special technique that involved quickly yanking the wood off

the roof of my car toward my head and then ducking so it could be loaded on my back, which worked great until my earring got caught and nearly delobed me). My toenail was black from dropping a drill on it, and my arms felt like jelly, and everything in between ached.

My guess is that my ears and limbs, back and butt would be less mangled if I'd had the courage to ask for help. For example, one day I was unloading lumber into the garage and accidentally knocked a door off its hinge. It was an old wood door that weighed a ton. I decided to reset it myself by hefting it up to a standing position and wrestling it into position across from the little pegs that held the hinge; I was spread-eagle with feet, arms, head, and a pry bar stretched as far as possible to properly angle the door. If this move was illustrated in a how-to book, it would be called "cat on a screen door" and would include multiple illustrations and a liability waiver.

I was sweating and grunting, making noises that I hadn't ever heard come out of my body, when my defibrillator fired. It sounded like the igniter on a range top, a *tcht, tcht, tcht, tcht, tcht,* and then it stopped. For some reason, I didn't let go (perhaps a primal instinct to avoid being laid flat by the door). I simply grimaced, clenched my teeth, and held on just like I had on the ladder with the skylight.

Some people would view this as a moment to catch their breath and back away, to call a friend or a door-hanging expert, but instead, I was mad at the door—at its size and my need for a fucking pry bar. I was pissed; if I had been a cartoon, my eyes would have spiraled and glowed red, and my body would have transformed to Hulkish proportions. Suddenly, I was imbued with superhuman strength, because I was able to lift the door and stick it back on its hinge, with a mighty *yawp* and then a big "Fuck you!" And then my defibrillator fired another series of shocks and I burst into tears.

Later, I told this story to my cardiologist and he explained that my defibrillator hadn't fired full-force; it had been quarter-force, a mechanism designed to pace me back into a normal rhythm (the equivalent of dropping a lit sparkler down your shirt, as opposed to a battery cable in a bathtub). I was relieved to learn that the box was equipped to sense my every move, but what the hell was I supposed to do when I got in a pinch?

"So what *did* you do?" my cardiologist asked, growing serious.

"I rehung the door and cussed it out," I said, "and then finished unloading the plywood."

I was stubborn like that, refusing to let my heart redefine how I operated. Looking back, there is a part of me that wants to replace the word *stubborn* with *reckless*; there are many things I would do differently now, but what good does it do to retrace your steps? Sometimes you simply do the things you do,

and it doesn't necessarily help to pick on the "old you" by pro-
claiming how smart the new you is.

Of course, out of necessity, I did occasionally ask for help.
After building my house, I tallied up the total cost: ten thousand dollars' worth of windows, wood, engineered metal straps,
the trailer, and a stupidly expensive solar electric system. But
that doesn't include the amount of money that I spent on beer
and pizza and coffee and muffins to support the hours of work
that I got from friends. They helped me lift the walls into place,
sheath the roof, build the kitchen cabinet, and insulate the
walls. One day, my friend Karen spent two hours planing old
barn wood so I could use it in the overhangs; the dust burned
her hands and left a red stain on her face outlining her respira-
tor. She looked like a scary clown for two days.

My friend Eileen kept me from going nuts by bringing me
burritos, pizza, coffee, and beer, and helped in lifting, sanding,
screwing, nailing, refastening, restaining, and remilling wood.
Now I wonder if she wasn't simply worried about me; all my
friends were worried about me, and I had cleverly shut down. If
someone asked how I was doing, I'd laugh and say, "Fantastic,"
and that was true. I really was having a blast figuring things
out, learning how to walk a four-foot skylight up a ladder in
flip-flops, and how to jury-rig a plug-in so I could test my electrical system. It was a huge amount of fun, and resting alongside that adventure was the way I sometimes stewed on my

diagnosis: congestive heart failure, the sort of disease that leaves you sleeping on the couch because you can't summon the energy to walk upstairs to your bedroom. It leaves your lungs filled with fluid, and so weak that you agree to move into your friends' living room, allowing them to set up a very nice articulated hospital bed because "it's the easiest and most comfortable way to do this."

I felt better when I didn't think about that stuff, when I focused on the fact that I could now lift a fifty-pound roll of tar paper like I was picking up the chairs in the kitchen to mop the floor. "Easy-peasy," I'd said as I pulled the last load of wood off the top of my car and stacked it in Camelli's garage. I was scared about getting sick and landing with hospice care in my friend's living room, lying there watching the ceiling fan while they ate dinner in the kitchen. It was better this way, me risking life and limb every day in the interest of my favorite project.

I couldn't have mustered the wherewithal to talk about my fear with my friends. Instead, I invited folks over for Southeast State Park functions: barbecues, bonfires, pizza and beer, an opportunity to play "who can donkey-kick the lawn chair the farthest" and "who can stand on one leg, bend over, and pick up a paper bag with their teeth the most number of times."

Only one friend seemed to gather enough courage to ask me point-blank about how I was sincerely doing with regard to my heart: my friend Lizzie, whom I'd known for years . . . since college; before she finished graduate school, law school, got married, and had kids. We were standing in my big kitchen, just before I finished the little house, and as we prepped burgers, slapping them in our palms like tiny baby bottoms, she asked me quietly, "Are you doing this because you're dying?"

"What? No-o-o-o," I stuttered as I flipped on the kitchen sink to wash my hands and find a pithy comeback. "No. I'm doing great; the little house is something I've always dreamed about. It's the midlife convertible I would have gotten if I was midlifed and could afford it."

"Deedles," she said, leaning into me by the sink, using the nickname she'd used when we were twenty years old and playing Frisbee in the park, "you know we love you. If you need anything, you can ask." She added this last part in a whisper, with her mouth barely inches from my ear.

I didn't know what to say, so I sputtered "Got it" as Lizzie reached past me and turned off the faucet. "Thank you," I offered, giving Liz a quick smile, and then grabbed the plate of burgers and walked out to the grill.

I couldn't imagine talking with my dearest, best friends about what had caused me to distance myself. They only saw that I was focused on details—lining up the screws along the sidewalls so they were all evenly spaced, using a level and tape measure to make sure the roof screws were properly aligned, and painting the shiny silver flashing a brick-red color so it wouldn't stand out around the windows. In my mind, it was all about the little things—the way the sun would likely catch and reflect the exposed metal straight back in your eyes when you least expected or wanted it—and controlling the final outcome.

A few weeks later, on Labor Day weekend, I was "done enough." The exterior was "buttoned up," as my carpenter friends would say when they were too tired to keep working and had sealed things up well enough to keep the weather out. The house looked gorgeous: just like an ad for pancake syrup or a painting called *A Simpler Time.*

The interior was insulated and sealed with knotty pine wall board but it still lacked window trim and kitchen shelves, and the little metal brackets that secured the front porch posts hadn't yet been trimmed out. I figured I'd get to that as soon as I landed in my new parking spot.

I'd spent a few nights in the little house, stretched out in my sleeping bag on a lawn chair cushion with my dog. I felt vulnerable sleeping there, like I was camped in my car and the neighbors were going to walk by in the night and see me drooling into my pillow. I also felt incredibly self-satisfied, remembering the day an East Indian man had stopped by with a camera, taking a photo of me in the loft as I shoved the blue-jean insulation into place, and remembering another day when a friend's little girl, Esmee, had practiced her hammering with a tiny wooden mallet, in synch with me pounding nails into the wallboards to hold them in place. I knew every square inch of this house. I *knew* it.

I fell asleep with a nearby streetlight leaking into the loft, outlining the way my muscular arm reached up and traced the form of the Big Dipper, the only constellation visible through the city's light pollution. I had done it.

"We made it," I whispered to RooDee, feeling her butt wedge against me to grab a bit more space on our cushion. "Now the adventure begins."

Who Cares If I
Appear Foolish?

(OLYMPIA, WASHINGTON, OCTOBER 2012)

I woke up this morning to a layer of frost on the skylight window. It was barely noticeable when I first opened my eyes, but as I lay there with the sun slowly pinking things up, I realized it looked like a Christmas tree had fallen on the roof. The crystals had formed into dozens of eight-to-ten-inch needled tapers, shooting off in all directions. I studied it, trying to put my finger on where I'd seen this before, and then I realized it was just like lying on my back when I was a kid, tucked under our family Christmas tree and looking up through the lights and ornaments.

I rolled on my side with the blankets over my head, and studied the frost like an art student studying a famous painting, like the twenty-year-old I used to be, when my teacher would send us off to the museum to study Van Gogh. I imagined that if I was still that girl, I'd balance my sketchbook on my lap now and attempt to pencil-draw each needle of frost. I'd start with the mass at the center of the window where the light seemed most intense, and work my way out to the edge where everything was melting. "Crap!" I blurted to my dog. I shot out from under the covers and tripped over myself trying to crawl across the bedding, trying to get out of the loft before the frost fully disappeared. I finally made it to the end of the bed, raced down the ladder, and a second later scampered back up with my camera, where I then hovered in the fog of my own breath as I snapped a photo called *The Christmas Tree*.

My dog had remained still through the entire affair, staring at me with her tail draped over her nose, but failing to uncurl her body as I knee-walked back to the window, camera in hand, crying, "Hey, would you look at that!"

The fact is, even after all these years of sleeping with my head inches from the roof, of rolling over day after day to see what's outside the skylight or on the skylight, after all this time and even though my dog has heard it all before, nature still surprises me. And then I'm surprised by my surprise, thinking that, at this stage of the game, I should be a bit bored by things like frost. In past winters, I've had frost that looked like fiddleheads, daggers, paisleys, martini picks, traditional snowflakes, dull wax paper, droopy wheat stalks, and sea kelp. The patterns on the east-side skylight, over the living room, were always different than those on the west side over my bed, and it seemed to me that there was some competition involved, like the windows were challenging each other to see who could create the most spectacular, supernatural effect in ice. I've taken photos of all of them to prove they once existed and to remind myself, later perhaps, when I'm preoccupied or stuck, or if I ever find myself doing dull little tasks inside a watery little office, that nature is stunning and that I was once happy living in a small house in winter.

For this same reason, I've tried to take photos of the light pouring in through the windows, hitting the opposite wall first thing in the morning. You can see the walls turn from wheat-colored to rose to amber, like the inside of a honey jug, but it takes a while, and my camera (which is also my cell phone *and* a flashlight, minicomputer, and construction level) can't filter the light change very well. It also can't pick up the subtle way frost or snow can look like the bottom of a Styrofoam cooler sitting on the skylight, or the way a big buildup of snow sounds like a bag of flour hitting the ground when it finally slides off the roof. My camera-phone can't capture what it smells like to walk into my house, or the way snow smells like a cotton ball, but I really wish it could. If my phone could capture odors, this morning I would have taken a picture of my dog's feet and the way they still smell like green grass and summer, even though everything has turned to mud outside.

The photos are pixelated and stored in my phone, and sometimes I'll forward them to my computer, where they're tucked neatly into a file that I've named "Photos." There's no further file organization beyond that; no smaller files labeled "Natural Wonders" or "Odd Things That Happen Sometimes," so someday when I want to find *The Christmas Tree*, I'll have to sort past *Spider in Keyhole*, *Sun in Earhole*, *Ants Carrying Cheese Puff*, and a hundred other photos. Most of the time, I appreciate the distraction and embrace it as an opportunity to revisit some of the more stunning things I've witnessed in the universe, but occasionally I'll just want to find the one damn photo, and that's when I'll question the value of keeping so many things, even if they're smaller than a frozen water molecule floating in cyberspace.

Years ago, in my big house, I probably would have enlarged and framed *The Christmas Tree*, and then I'd have tucked the clunky framed photo on the shelf near the fireplace, where I'd occasionally look at it and feel satisfied with myself. It would sit next to photos of my dog at the ocean and my friends looking impish, and would complement the various houseplants and books that littered the shelves.

There was a large painting that towered above the fireplace, resting on top of the mantel because I couldn't find a way to hang it on the brick wall. It showed a rotund naked lady sitting in a chair with her head resting on her hand and her eyes closed like she'd just dozed off—the pose you'd strike sitting at the doctor's office or while waiting for an overdue train, only naked.

The picture came from a friend who had purchased it from an art student, who had probably sold all his artwork to fund a trip to Europe. He had created it in a portrait class, stretching the canvas himself, painting the naked lady, and then banging together a wood frame to finish it out. It had a "just finished" feel to it that made it unpretentious but at the same time more dynamic than anything else I'd seen. Maybe it was the color or shadows, the paint layers, or simply the way the lady slumped in the chair like a perfect sigh; whatever the reason, it didn't take much imagination to think that, at any second, the model might come alive. She'd open her eyes and do a sleepy stretch, arms extended, rib cage expanded so her breasts grew to the size of trash can lids, then she'd lean forward, grab her robe, arise, and walk out of the frame.

I had nearly cried when I handed the painting off to a friend, and again when I took down the paintings in the dining room and living room, pieces that were gifts from friends, along with my own work. It was hard to fathom that anyone would enjoy this artwork as much as I had—that they'd understand the beauty in my friend John's illustration of an exploding stick of dynamite, or the story behind my pencil drawing called *Girl Running with Scissors*—so I packaged up the pieces and later slid them into Candyce and Paula's attic for storage. Months later, when they invited me to dinner, I walked in and found that they'd rummaged through the attic and rehung most of the artwork in their own living room. They were worried I'd be angry, but instead I was shocked and relieved—it was like finding your family wrapped in emergency blankets after a daring rescue at sea.

I had no idea that "letting go" would be so complicated; that it would sometimes feel liberating and other times more sorrowful and lonely. In the long run, most of it was like standing on the shore, watching your family set sail for America, and they're smiling and waving good-bye, and getting smaller and smaller, but you are still the same size with no one to talk to.

I managed the artwork in late August, saving it for last, after parting with my furniture, the rugs, garden tools, and kitchenware. When I finally got around to the stuff on the walls, the floors were already empty.

Culling through my books was the hardest. I had hundreds—novels and biographies, a full set of art encyclopedias, poetry anthologies, home repair manuals, travel guides, schoolbooks, and journals that I'd schlepped along on backpacking trips, kayaking, and back and forth to university. They were my companions, friends who had moved with me from one house to another, from one state to another, over mountain passes into Olympia for six years, then south to Portland and the Willamette Valley for another six. They had entertained me late at night, put me to sleep, made me laugh or cry, or made me feel normal.

Books had rescued me when I most needed saving, like when I was visiting my parents and wanted to appear too busy to answer their questions about why I had broken up with my last "special someone," as my mom liked to say. Books had sustained me when I was too sick to do anything but lounge about on the couch in the living room, when I wondered what might be the last thing in my mind as I drifted toward my own death: maybe the image of a boat being kicked away from the shore with an endless blue sky above and the sea spreading out forever, just like a scene in a Hemingway novel.

They had been the things that I'd stood on, sometimes literally, but more often, when I wanted to see how to repair the kitchen sink or rewire the bathroom, or was attempting a complicated remodel of the old plaster walls in the downstairs bedroom. Books were smarter than me and words inspired me. I still think that Diane Ackerman's poem challenged me to build a little house in the first place—to try something new, charge forward without a clear understanding of what would happen next, because: "given something like death, what does it matter if one looks foolish now and then, or tries too hard, or cares too deeply?"

In the end, Thoreau, Whitman, Hafiz, and a dozen other writers put me up to the task of seeing if I dared to "live a life worth living." They left me no choice but to pull the rug (along with the couch and all the other furniture) out from under my old normal life, which, sadly, at that moment included letting go of my mentors, their words, and their books, so I could put my faith in the good old-fashioned public library.

It took me a long time to sort through the bookshelves. At first, I thumbed through each volume, reading the little notes scribbled in the margins, and gently placing each book in a box. But after a while, as the gravity of saying good-bye wore me out and I was able to pick up the pace, I could focus on the task at hand, as if I were working in a slaughterhouse, where there was nothing left to do but keep pace, grab the book off the shelf, throw it in the box, repeat, and hope the day would end soon enough. It was horrible, and it made me think of the way my mother had hugged me extra hard but was otherwise stiff, and almost mean, on the day I loaded myself into my car for the move from the Midwest to the Pacific Northwest and my new home. I had no idea, until now, how my leaving must have weighed on her.

I didn't plan for this sort of hardship; I thought getting rid of stuff would be a simple matter of elbow grease and logic. Feelings of loss or remorse weren't supposed to be a factor, because the real adventure was in building the little house—in operating power tools and going to the lumberyard and finding my way through the aisles of metal fasteners, brackets, house wrap, and wood. I thought there wouldn't be any emotion left after refastening the rafters for the third time. I thought I would be beyond all of that.

I had earmarked a full weekend to crank through the entire house, imagining that I could pare things down to their least common denominators: basic necessities (like a good kitchen knife, a pillow, and underwear) and stuff that I appreciated but could survive without for the next few months and possibly forever. I figured it would take a few minutes to sort through the kitchen drawers, chock-full of mismatched silverware, old twisty-ties, and utensils that I couldn't recall ever using. I imagined it would be easy to slide things into garage-sale boxes and to sort the stuff that was functional and not too badly stained from the stuff that needed a good washing or, sadly, was destined for the landfill.

Within a few minutes of my kitchen job, I realized I was in trouble. I stumbled upon the pantry where my housemates and I had shoved our canned goods: abandoned pinto beans, spaghetti sauce, old Chex cereal, rice, and dried spices. It was like staring through a telescope at the galaxy, with a spiraling nebula of canned peaches and a supernova of plastic baggies full of oats, lentils, quinoa, wheat berries, and pasta. It made me feel small. "Lard help me," I muttered as I threw out unused Crisco. I pawed through the lot, examining the labels and wondering which one of my housemates over the years had purchased canned okra and pickled beets, only to realize it had been me, which launched me into a full-scale review of every can, searching for the expiration date and wondering if it was possible to get food poisoning from a can of four-year-old chili. I felt horrible within the first ten minutes of the first day of the first month of my cleanout. "What was I thinking?" I lamented as I grabbed the little hand-crank can opener and started cleaving open all the expired canned goods and dumping their guts into the compost.

It took me hours of mind-numbing work to sort through the pantry, and then there was the rest of the house: the attic, the basement, garage, and yard, which proved to be just as difficult. The basement was full of old house paint, rollers, plumbing supplies and building materials, ski equipment, golf clubs, climbing gear, kayaking stuff. There was a cabinet full of boatbuilding material, expensive fiberglass cloth, resin, brass fittings, ring-shank nails, and paint—stuff that was so expensive, I sort of wanted to punch it for leaving me with such a difficult chore.

In the end, it took me months (time interrupted by work and house building . . . but months!) to go through all my belongings, and I can't even remember what happened to most of this stuff; I only remember that all of it had to go and I wanted to keep it. It was agonizing. There was some consolation in giving things away to people I knew, instead of loading them into a Goodwill box, so early on I got a roll of masking tape and started labeling boxes: "John and Brenda" or "Chinn and Fritz," and anyone else I could imagine who might enjoy a box of bathroom tiles, a set of art encyclopedias, or a bag filled with stinky cotton balls (largely pulled out of vitamin bottles) hat could be made into a nice-looking Santa beard at Christmas.

In the attic, I leaned into the roof rafters and balanced on a flimsy piece of plywood between the joists as I sifted through letters, photos, flattened roses, little boxes with seashells and rocks, an arrowhead, newspaper clippings, and the like. I hardly ever looked at this stuff, and I couldn't believe how easily it dragged me back to the moments when I was a high school student, a runner, Rob's fiancée, a rock climber, Chinn's best friend, an aunt, a goofball, a hot-air balloonist, a dutiful daughter . . . all these things that used to define me and in some cases still did.

As I browsed the photos, I remembered Rob, my ex-fiancé, calling me months after we broke up, ringing me in the middle of a New Year's Eve party to tell me that he was burning everything I had ever given him. He had such a sweet soft voice, asking if I wanted to get the things he'd given me so we could ceremonially burn them together in different cities, as a sign of letting go. I imagined him standing in his parka and snow boots, marching up to a barbecue loaded with letters, our wedding invitations, and photos. It made me cry, and as I stood on my back porch with the phone pressed tight to one ear, my finger in the other ear to hear over the sound of the party, so I could tell him, "It's New Year's Eve here, and raining, and a fire would never light." Things had ended so terribly, and I couldn't fathom the idea of torching the little that remained.

"Okay. Good-bye," he said, soft and kind, and then *click*. I heard from my folks a few months later that he was engaged to a nurse.

Now, sitting in my attic, I leaned back into the rafters and sighed, and then sobbed as I loaded a box of things to burn in my backyard bonfire pit. After a few minutes, I picked up speed. "But I am alive," I whispered. I culled through the box and kept a few things (who was I if I didn't have at least one good love letter addressed solely to me?) but got rid of the bulk, imagining that this was exactly the sort of stuff that was shoved in storage units and attics all across America, and the stuff that ends up in a different state, stuck to a rosebush after a tornado.

As I cleaned out the house, I faced a thousand near crying fits. I'd come across some forgotten knickknack, and all of a sudden it seemed I could feel the pressure inside my body change. Things would grow still then, followed by a cloudburst. Other times, it felt more like a light rain, like something that would hit the windshield of my chore list, sprinkling an otherwise perfectly sunny day. It's a little embarrassing to admit what I cried over, but here's the truth: I teared up when I put the Whirley Pop popcorn popper in a stack of things to go. It wasn't the popcorn, it was the way Holly and Sam would sing in unison, "Whirley Pop, Whirley Pop, we're making it pop with Whirley Pop." They'd sing that while heating the popcorn kernels over the stovetop and twisting a little crank that kept the kernels moving around inside the pot. They were hilarious in their excitement for Whirley Pop popcorn.

Along with all the crying fits were equal squalls of unbridled giddiness. I found and then mailed odd curios to my friends, like the pair of giant red clown shoes I mailed to my friend Chinn that I discovered in my basement and then forwarded along with a little note that said, "I saw these and thought of you." There was a set of Christmas lights that I had made one year—a set of plastic baby doll heads that lit up like something out of a horror film—that was a perfect gift for my friend Mike, whose wife and kids continue to drape them on the tree every year as a memorial to "crazy Deezus" (their nickname for me). Every time I'd find one of these little gems and mail it off, I'd laugh. And then the ensuing phone conversations, after the gift had been received, were enough to double me up.

Moving was hard, but not impossibly horrid, and in fact, over the long haul I found it incredibly liberating. After a short bit of time, it became more like stripping naked on the beach, kicking off your clunky shoes and pulling your shirt off while simultaneously using your foot like a hand to yank off your socks, preparing for the way the warm sea will feel against every dimple and fold of your body. Letting go of "stuff" allowed the world to collapse behind me as I moved, so I became nothing more or less than who I simply was: Me.

Hobo-A-Go-Go

I called my dad this morning to wish him a happy Thanksgiving, to explain how much I love him and that he's the best. We chatted about the weather and how I haven't made much progress on my book lately because I've been doing things like power-washing the neighbor's carport. Ultimately, half an hour into our conversation, I realized we weren't talking about how much I appreciate him, but instead were yammering about his leaking toilet. We were father-daughter bonding over the best way to reset the bowl on a wax ring, and how you have to dangle the toilet awkwardly over the open sewer hole before dropping it like a cinder block on the wax ring to seal things up. He sounded exhausted by the process.

"Forget about it, Pop. I'll get it when I fly back."

This is how it goes with many of my friends. We'll start out talking about something normal like the way so-and-so's kid has pinkeye or the way our dogs sniff butts, but somewhere in the mix I'll find myself explaining how to repair a hot water heater. To be honest, I'd prefer to talk about hot water heaters, which is why I'm bored at baby showers, and why I feel alienated by many Hollywood movies where the plot is focused on looking sexy and getting laid. I prefer to watch a YouTube clip about the honey badger, or videos that show you how to reload the whip line in a weed eater.

I used to try harder to fit in with my friends who liked to discuss their OKCupid online dating experience, or how a good pedicure can save your life. I'd lean in and tilt my head with determined interest, and then compliment her on the color of her toenails and ask for the name of her pedicurist; or I'd fuss over the way my friend had just poached an egg, and suggest that he could be a master chef for the president because of the way the yoke isn't runny and the white part doesn't feel rubbery. But the truth is, I'm a complete ding-dong when it comes to many normal activities. I don't know anything about poached eggs and I'm even more at a loss if the conversation turns to feelings, for example if someone wants to know how I'm doing. "How is your health?" they might ask.

I'd rather talk about my new lawn mower: how it starts every time without having to prime the engine, and it's got a way to hook a garden hose to the housing so you can quickly clean the blade and undercarriage. "It's genius," I might boast to my coworkers, who would then sigh (or yawn) and walk to the copy machine.

I've always been this way, and I'm not alone. The day before I left Portland, I ended up talking with a guy about the Ford F-250 that I'd just purchased. He and I had talked before; he was a regular at the same coffee shop I frequented, and when he casually asked me how I was doing, I mentioned I was getting ready to move my house for the first time. This launched us into an hour-long conversation about the benefits of a Power Stroke engine, diesel fuel, and manual versus automatic transmissions. He walked back to the house with me to look at the rig, and to make suggestions for the best way to back up the truck and connect it to the house.

"Big move," he offered, pausing and staring at the house.

"Yeah. Big move." I sighed and smiled. I suddenly considered bursting into tears and leaning into this strange know-it-all. I'd ask him, "What was I thinking?" and he'd shush me and tell me everything was going to be all right. But I didn't do that, and instead kept my hands in my pockets and asked, "Hey, what kind of gas mileage do you think I'll get with this rig?"

The route was a tricky thing, and something I'd pored over and prepared for for weeks. I had driven the route from Portland to Olympia a thousand times over the years, but hadn't ever much noticed what was what until moving the little house became a reality. I started taking notes: "Mile marker (MM) 22, cross wind from river; MM 45, right lane piece of shit." I noted the location of rest stops, bridges, overpasses, and truck stops; and as I got into Olympia, I tracked the location of low-hanging utility lines and tree branches, and thought about how to best navigate streetlights and turnabouts.

I went into the Department of Motor Vehicles in Portland to pick up a license plate, and explained to the clerk that I had just finished building a tiny house on wheels. As I spoke, I gestured with the international symbol for home—my hands coming together to resemble a roof—and smiled very big. I was so excited, I even showed the clerk a photo of the house. The lady looked at me and then at my paperwork without saying a word. She had me write a check for the plate and tabs, and sent me on my way with plate number 978-RV. And just like that, I was ready to hit the road. But I wasn't.

I was scared. I wanted someone else to do it for me; to come hook up the truck so everything would be all right—hitch, chains, lights, brakes, emergency "breakaway," side mirrors, lug nuts, spare tires, axles, rocker arms, springs, road flares, tire wrench, tire tread, tire pressure gauge . . . everything. I wanted someone else to move the house, to know by feel that a tire was losing pressure, or by some bit of barely visible movement or some hardly audible sound that the house was wiggling loose. I wanted them to arrive safely in Olympia, to drive the house to its resting spot, and to set it in place. And once they got there, I'd arrive with a beer and we'd celebrate all our heroics.

Instead, what I had was the next-best thing: my friends Candyce and Paula agreed to follow me to Olympia in their car, acting as scouts to watch for any potential problems. "We'll brush up on our truck-driver follow-car lingo," they offered.

I moved my tools into the living room of the little house, parking them next to a couple of small armchairs, a houseplant named Virgil, a box of kitchenware, and a few books. My clothes were tucked in the closet, fitting easily in a space smaller than the file cabinet I kept at work, and my bed was laid out on the loft floor for the trip. Everything fit precisely, tucking into hidden drawers that were built into the toe-kick below the kitchen counter, or into one of the two wicker baskets that I'd salvaged from Goodwill to contain socks, underwear, headbands, down booties, mittens, and a felted elf (a tiny three-inch character with a lumpy head and pipe-cleaner arms) that was a gift from a friend's daughter and would now be making the big trip to Olympia in the basket, to later become a sort of gatekeeper in my window. Even Buster, my thirty-pound ceramic pig, who had been parked outside my old house for years, sitting like a smiling cinder block on the front porch, was able to squeeze into the little house for the ride to Olympia. Once we arrived, I'd drag him out to sit on the porch and continue his watch for visitors.

My big house was empty, nothing left except for the booming echo in the living room and telltale paint dribbles on the floor from a year or two (or three) ago. There were gouges in the door frames from moving furniture, and little bite marks on the trim from when RooDee was a puppy, entertaining herself in the kitchen while I was away at work. There was the spot near the back door where I was standing when my dad called to tell me that my mom had been in a terrible accident, and the other spot where my brother called to tell me he and his wife were expecting their first baby. I had made out with my most recent sweetie in the backyard, the kitchen, the living room, bedroom, and bathroom; and we had broken up standing in the driveway. My friend Meg had laughed so hard one night that she literally peed her pants, dropping her cards and rushing off to the bathroom as the rest of our group howled and shook our heads on the table.

I loved that house, and everything it brought me—both good and bad.

The day before we left, Candyce and Paula helped me hook up the little house and move it from the driveway onto the street, and we walked through the things that could go wrong— wobbly wheels, roofing that appeared to vibrate, sudden listing or leaning, or any odd fishtail movements of the trailer. We practiced using our cell phones like walkie-talkies, with me hunkered in the pickup truck in front of the house while they sat behind it in their car.

I offered in a serious tone (a tone I hardly ever used, but I was freaked out enough by the idea of moving the house that this seemed critically important): "Candyce and Paula, are there any problems?" I sounded both apprehensive and wishful.

To which they responded: "Um, not to distract from the moment, but I think you're supposed to announce yourself before you ask a question. That's what you'd do if you were a truck driver on the open highway. You're supposed to say something like 'Charlie Bravo Niner-Niner, this is The Big Tiny, pedal to the metal, what's the skinny on this little woody?' That's what you're supposed to say."

"What?" I asked as I got out of my truck and walked back toward their car, coming around the corner of my house to see them laughing and holding the phone out between them.

They continued, not noticing me walking up to the car: "Charlie Bravo, you're supposed to announce yourself, offer a question, and then we say something like 'Tango Nacho, this is the red bucket of goods [their car was red]. Check. Check. You got your bumper sticker in place [that would be them]. Clean and green to go. Ready to hit a double nickel all the way to OlyWa. Over.'"

I stood staring at them as they laughed, and walked up and leaned in on the driver's door. "Over 'n' out," Candyce mumbled, contorting her mouth toward the phone while staring at me. She gave me a big shit-eating grin, which totally cracked me up, and the three of us laughed like that for ten minutes.

That night, we had a going-away party. My friends showed

up from all over town, with friends of friends, neighbors, and folks from the coffee shop. People walked in carrying food and their camping gear—folding chairs, nesting plates, forks, and pocketknives to replace the kitchenware that was now all missing from my house; some brought the glasses that I'd handed off to them, for one last hurrah around the backyard fire pit. We ate an exquisite meal and hung out in Southeast State Park, and then, as it got dark, we all walked out to the little house to christen its maiden voyage.

Someone handed me a bottle of champagne and I cracked it over the ball hitch of the trailer, smashing it, hooting, and encouraging everyone to run circles around the rig. We all whooped and laughed as we raced with one hand on the truck, the house, and then the truck again.

At eight the next morning, a bunch of us met on the front lawn of the big house. People came with bells, pots and pans, and other makeshift noisemakers. One neighbor (a guy whom I hadn't met until the night before) offered me a copy of his favorite book; another gave me a bouquet of flowers, and someone else hung a giant poster across the back of the little house, a modified "Wide Load" sign reading: "CUTE LOAD."

My friend Kimo—the new owner of the big house—showed up, just like she had the night before. She brought a small notebook inscribed with a quotation from Walt Whitman: "My ties and ballasts leave me/my elbows rest in the sea-gaps/I skirt sierras/my palms cover continents/I am afoot with my vision."

"Good luck, Deedles." She smiled.

We gave hugs all around and I loaded into the truck while Candyce and Paula crawled into their car. This was it.

I drove away listening to a parade of wooden spoons being banged on pots; they chased me up the street, cheering, making me feel like a champion, like I'd donated a kidney to the neighborhood and now I was off.

As I passed the coffee shop, I honked the horn at the folks waving good-bye and I saw some of the neighbors running, pushing their kids in strollers and holding pots and pans, racing to get to the intersection to wish me well. That was the moment I lost it. I completely broke down crying, realizing everything was changing. I was moving. Leaving. Pulling up stakes and heading to Olympia, and I had no idea what I was doing. I was flying blind, trusting everything would work out all right.

Ten minutes into our commute, Paula called to let me know the back door had swung open. She was deadpan and all business, and at the next intersection, I ran back and dead-bolted the door.

A half hour into our commute, we pulled off the highway into a rest stop where I could double-check the lug nuts and cross chains as the Russians had advised. I was bending down near the wheel well when one of the largest men I'd ever met walked up to me and asked what I was pulling. "It's my house," I said. "I built it myself."

"Whaaaaaaat!" he exclaimed. "Well, aren't you something. I could use a little cabin like this for hunting."

Before I knew it, there was a small gathering of people, peeping in the windows and crawling down on hands and knees to see underneath the house. One lady asked to have her picture taken next to me while standing in front of the house, and another remarked (and I think she really thought she was giving me a genius idea at no charge) that "this li'l thing would make a perfect food cart for selling sausages or some other old-timey cabin food at a fair!"

"Ya." I smiled as I loaded RooDee into the truck. "But y'know, the windows are too small. I'd chip the dishware handing food out to customers."

We inched back onto the highway, and at the first overpass, Candyce and Paula pulled far behind, backing up a fair distance to see how the house handled the overhead concrete bridge. I was fairly certain I'd built it to squeeze below the overpass, but at times I had been a bit fast and loose with my tape measure, so there was room for doubt. A quarter mile away, I floored the engine, slamming my flip-flop onto the accelerator and racing from 55 miles an hour to 60, then 70, believing that moving faster through an obstruction would somehow save me. At the last minute, I ducked my head into my armpit, wondering if I'd hear the splinter of wood and metal exploding as it hit the overpass. But nothing happened;

my gas tank drained a little lower, and the little house and I continued.

The cab of the truck was huge, and every bump jolted me forward, leaving me feeling like I was ten years old again, driving our old hay truck across the fields as my dad, mom, and sister bucked hay bales into the back. I pulled RooDee closer on the bench seat, and alternated between crying and laughing as I scream-sang old Queen songs to bolster my courage: "WE WILL, WE WILL ROCK YOU . . ." for ten miles, shifting in my seat; "WE ARE THE CHAMPIONS, MY FRIENDS . . . AND WE'LL KEEP ON FIGHTING TO THE END . . ." for another ten.

We made it into Olympia just after lunch, and parked the house in a vacant lot tucked into a neighborhood of large houses. It felt like we'd been traveling for weeks, like I'd been living on bread and water, and now here I was in the Promised Land, which was really just a lot that belonged to Candyce's ex-brother-in-law, who had agreed to let me stay on his property in exchange for weeding the garden. This would be home for the next week, while I prepped my final landing spot on the other side of town.

The lot was huge—three or four acres large—and the sort of place that could hold a whole subdivision of small houses. It looked like a state park, with eighty-foot fir trees, fruit trees, and a wide-open field that emptied out to a distant tree-lined fence. There was a circle drive that terminated next to the foundation of an old farmhouse that had burned down, and a grape arbor that framed the spot perfectly.

"Holy Samoly!" I screamed as I crawled out of the truck, dripping sweat and slightly hoarse from the trip. "This is awesome!"

RooDee raced around the property, chasing squirrels, while we leveled the house with jacks. I put things away inside the house, standing the loft ladder in place and placing the teakettle over the stove. It felt so good to be standing in the house; a real house with real windows that looked out at Olympia, and a real bed that I'd put together in the loft. I stood for a second, admiring how beautiful it was, every inch, like I was seeing it for the first time.

That night, my friend Brad came over to check out my house. He had been a friend for years and more recently had been giving me acupuncture treatments for my heart. He was also a tiny-house nut and couldn't wait to see the real deal.

The solar electric system wasn't turned on yet, so as it got dark I gave him a tour of the house by headlamp, showing him the wood countertop, kitchen sink, compost toilet, sleeping loft, and the tiny window that opened up over the bed. We sat outside for a couple of hours, using a small candle as a bonfire; first listening to the bats whiz around scooping up bugs, and then smelling the woodsmoke from someone else's fire.

Brad asked how it felt to finally be here, to be done, and I said, "Amazing. Like I just delivered a four-thousand-pound baby and someone should write an article about it for the *Journal of Medicine*." I chortled, and made fake cooing sounds at my front porch while I stroked the porch post like a baby. And then something weird happened: I started to cry.

I prefer to cry alone . . . in the car, in the shower, in bed, or in the bathroom stall at work where I can simultaneously cry and dig my fingernails into the toilet paper roll. So, as soon as I started crying, I wanted it to stop, which resulted in me holding my breath as Brad stared at his shoes, perhaps wishing he hadn't asked how I was doing.

I closed my eyes and willed the tears to dry up. I didn't want Brad to watch me cry so hard it looked like I was going to barf, and maybe he should hold my hair out of my face; to watch me cry so desperately he would wonder if there was something wrong with him for never having cried that hard. I didn't need that; I was a champion, my friend, so I regained my composure and gently laid my hand on Brad's, cracking a joke about how exhausted I was from getting in and out of the truck (a massive step that required a high-jump scissor kick to land on the seat).

I *was* a champion. I felt it everywhere—in my arches, the balls of my feet, my calves and shins; I felt it in my viscera, in my body pulpy, and in my arteries, which were currently carrying blood toward the bruise I'd made when I fell through the front door of my new house just after we'd arrived at the field. In that case, I had reached for a water bottle sitting in the kitchen sink, but I lost my footing on the doorjamb and fell, stopping my fall with my ulna—the sturdy bottom bone connecting my wrist and my elbow, which had been breaking my falls since childhood. I had arrived, as if I'd conquered the impossible; as if I'd traveled across two mountain passes and eighteen hundred miles, carrying my children half the distance while my husband walked the ox and our covered wagon on ahead. And now all that remained was putting a bow on this perfect little package. Tomorrow I'd drive over to my soon-to-be-permanent home site, a lumpy place that required a rototiller to level things out, and I'd work on making things smooth and welcoming, and maybe tomorrow night I would sit on these same steps and feel less lost.

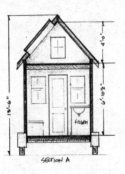

SECTION A

There Goes the
Neighborhood

I used obtuse language and a certain cheekiness to ferret out a place to park my house; it's what I'd been doing for years, as, for example (and because this really happened), if I was free for Thanksgiving dinner, I might cackle into the phone, "It's snowing out and I have a new saucer sled. If you'll save a bit of that turkey fat, we can take things to a whole new level!" which was followed by an invitation to Thanksgiving dinner and a postdinner sledding event that was unparalleled in hilarity. It wasn't that I had called specifically to be invited to dinner, but I certainly appreciated having that door opened. This is what my bachelor friends do all the time with laundry, food, and home decorating.

Something similar happened with regard to my house when

I proposed via e-mail, "Ha-ha, wouldn't it be funny if when I finished my house, I parked it in your backyard?" Two sets of friends, Candyce and Paula (whose living room had become my bedroom during the months I had driven back and forth to Olympia) and Hugh and Annie (who had repeatedly invited me to Christmas and Thanksgiving dinner with or without a sled) had taken the bait and offered me their yards.

I walked the back lot on Candyce and Paula's property. They had a weedy spot near their chicken coop where I could park my house and attempt to ignore the clamor from the neighborhood playground. It would be difficult to back the house into this spot; the accessing alley was grown over with apple trees and blackberries, and in fact, I couldn't even find the alley until Candyce pointed it out.

A few weeks before I finished the house, I had taken a walk with Annie around Capitol Lake in Olympia, and as RooDee dove in and out of the cattails along the swampy shore, Annie turned and asked where I was going to park my little house. "Oh," I joked, "I'm planning to put it in your backyard." She laughed along with me, and a few minutes later dropped her voice. "We really hope you do."

After our walk, I drove up the hill and perused their backyard. I walked down the access alley and surveyed the way it ran between two sets of fenced backyards, with Hugh and Annie's lot on one side and a duplex with a kiddie pool on the other. It was workable, and the corner lot where Annie imagined I could park was nice, albeit a bit close to Aunt Rita's house.

Even though I'd visited Hugh and Annie's house a thousand times, and celebrated some holidays and birthdays at Rita's, I'd never noticed how compact their living arrangement seemed to be. Their houses were connected by a patio and a carport, thirty feet of common airspace, a lilac bush, and a massive hundred-foot fir tree that sat between the houses like the mast of a ship.

Somehow, the snug fit seemed workable, in the way that you might feel fine wearing a pair of overly tight jeans to a party, knowing everything would work out as it should in the end (fingers crossed).

I trusted Hugh and Annie in a way that made it seem okay to blurt out one day at Mark and Shelly's house, as I was reading through the restrictions on Mark's medications, "Hey, I'm also taking a medication that says you have to clean the feeding tube every time you administer the drug. HA!" I giggled and then looked up over my glasses, staring at Hugh and Annie, who had been in the middle of some other odd task, while Shelly was off with Mark and the boys were upstairs.

Annie gave me a look, inviting me to say more, and then simply said, "Your heart?"

"Ya," was all I said.

They knew the story. I'd shared my prognosis but not in detail; I had explained things more in the way you'd list recipe ingredients, "heart, arrhythmia, defibrillator, medication, enlarged heart, failing." And then I'd made a joke. I can't remember that, but I'm sure it is true.

Days after our walk around Capitol Lake, I had called Hugh and Annie to ask about their backyard, and whether they were serious. Hugh offered that they had checked with the cartel—Rita, Keeva, and Kellen—and had then also talked with the neighbors and the laws of reason; everyone was on board.

So here I sat in a temporary open lot—a beautiful field circled by fir trees in Olympia, Washington—ready to venture over to Hugh and Annie's house tomorrow to start Operation Get Here Now, as Annie was calling it.

////////////////////////

Day two at Hugh and Annie's house, we rolled away a section of the cyclone fence to let me back the house in from the alley. We then dragged in the rototiller so I could mulch the soil and level it out, and plow under the tall grass, old mint, and the small ant farms and bug cities that had assumed control of Hugh and Annie's garden when they abandoned it a few years before. It was a massive production, and all the while I could see Rita sitting just inside her house, staring at me through the screen door.

"It'll be a discombobulated mess in that corner over there

for only a little while," I'd told Rita, "and then we'll all get used to it." She squinted at me as I spoke, partially because her eyesight was failing due to macular degeneration, but also because her backyard had been turned into a brown scab—a lumpy, weeping spot with part of the fence missing, which, even though this was a safe place, made the entire compound feel vulnerable.

"Humm," she offered, and nodded.

While she watched, I leveled a little pad formerly occupied by thatching ants and some yellow-jacket wasps, and then brought in a load of wood chips to keep the place from turning into a mud swamp when the weather changed.

Meanwhile, my little house remained in the vacant lot across town. I tended to the owner's garden, and walked the perimeter of the property to explore the old grape arbor, the blackberry vines, an old quince tree, and amazing three-foot-diameter fir trees. I loved it there except for the occasional feeling at night, when I'd struggle out of bed and stumble down the ladder, being guided by moonlight and the way I knew (I *knew*) every square inch of the house, to pee in my toilet, which was nothing more than a glorified bucket with sawdust littering my deposits. It was weird, and also comfortable. This was the new normal.

Finally, Hugh and Annie's lot was ready to receive us, so I drove over using the back roads; the city streets I'd selected because they didn't include too many low-hanging branches or power lines and no squirreling intersections where a long (and "cute") load would be at risk of smashing into a fire hydrant, decorative rock wall, or other hazards. I was giddy! I had made it over a hundred miles, around fifty curves, wind shears, bumps, and vibrations, and the little house had performed masterfully.

And then I rolled around the corner and hit my first tight spot: the entrance to the alley that would deliver me to my new backyard. It was blocked by an old sweet gum tree with knobby, low-hanging limbs.

Candyce, Annie, Hugh, Keeva, and Kellen gathered rakes and brooms to lift the branches high as I passed. I grabbed a tree saw from behind my truck seat, one of the few old house tools that I had kept, and without much fanfare I scrambled up the tree, steadied myself on a low limb, and whacked off a few choice branches—nothing too crazy, so as not to piss off the tree owner (I hoped). With that, I started to maneuver the house down the alley with a thumbs-up and then a big "Whoa whoa whoa" from Hugh. One branch, the real knob-knocker of them all, was about to peel the skylight off my roof, so I climbed the tree again, but this time with a ratcheting rope in tow. I slowly cranked the branch out of the way, yanking it closer to a branch a bit higher in the tree, and then released it once the house had squeezed by.

Twenty minutes later, after I had sweated a small lake of water into my T-shirt, my little house found its place in the backyard, nestled near the juniper bushes and the neighbor's chain-link fence. I set up my solar panels a few feet away from the house, pigtailing them into the electric panel that I'd installed inside the house below my locker-size closet, and I leveled the house with my truck jack and cinder blocks. The whole operation took less than an hour. Hugh and I set a couple of platform steps off the front porch, and we all gathered around, chatting and laughing. RooDee curled up next to Rita, her new best friend, and as the sun went down, my friends dispersed. I opened a beer, and parked myself on the front porch with my back against the door. Out of nowhere, a pinging sound erupted ten feet above my head, causing me to duck and giggle—bats. I knew the sound from our family farm as a kid but I hadn't heard it in years.

Finally, I was home.

Modern Conveniences

(OLYMPIA, WASHINGTON, DECEMBER 2012)

Nothing much has changed over the past several years. If you compared a series of satellite photos from 2004 up to the current day, you'd see that my little house has been perched in roughly the same spot from the start, looking like a small, shiny outbuilding, a shed maybe, tucked in the corner along the fence and back alley. Depending on the day the photos were taken, you might also see a blurry pink dot, which would be me, dashing across the lawn, wearing nothing but a bath towel, scuttling from Rita's back door to my house after a shower. It hasn't happened very often—maybe half a dozen times in eight years—but that is exactly the sort of behavior (the one-in-a-millionth moment, the one time you dropped your guard) that finds its way into a photo.

Rita's shower has one of those fancy adjustable heads, where you twist it one way and the water jets out ballistically, or twist it another and the water blobs out gently. I prefer the squishy water, but the other day I made a switch to see if the water-pick setting would remove construction adhesive from my hair. I was standing there with my head under the jet stream, with my fingers in my ears and my eyes shut (a protective posture), when I realized the shower noise inside my head was exactly like the storm noise inside my house a few nights before.

It was the first big rainstorm of the season, with wind blowing in and shooting rain at the roof like marbles, then rock salt, then frozen grapes, then a fire hydrant. It slammed into the house in waves, delivering a freakish amount of water, left to right and then back to front. The house rocked with the bigger wind gusts, making it impossible to go back to sleep, and making me wonder if the house was slowly being pushed toward the center of the yard.

At one point, the rain was thudding so hard I seriously considered the possibility that fish were falling on the roof. I'd read this could happen: fish scooped into a waterspout, a small tornado at sea, only to land a hundred miles inland; not a crazy idea, given the fact that Puget Sound was less than a mile away—just down the hill—and likely rising by the minute.

Lightning struck somewhere west of my neighborhood, and the giant flash of light gave me a chance to sit up and notice that the neighbor's tree was bending sideways away from the wind. This was about the time that RooDee started panting and shaking, keeping her eyes on me and her ears flat to her head, whining at me like the bed was too small a lifeboat. That was also the moment that I remembered I hadn't reconnected the grounding wire to my electrical system.

"Shit!" I yelped. "Shitty shit shit!"

The grounding cable was about as big around as my pinky finger, and normally connected the solar electric system (the battery, inverter, meter, and panels) to a copper post that was pounded four feet into the ground. This was supposed to keep the system from frying if it got hit by lightning, and now ("Oh shit!") I realized I hadn't reconnected the cable after moving things around the other day. I had disconnected the wire while wrestling the solar panels into a new position in the yard, a spot near the brown scab of my garden—a spot that was bleeding a few weeks ago but now looked painful to the touch. At the time, I imagined that I was smart and clever for optimizing my position under the sun, but now I was screwed; the panels were lined with metal and sat ten feet above the ground like a giant two-thousand-dollar lightning rod.

"Not so smart! Not so smart!" I whined at RooDee while staring out the window.

I had labored over whether or not I even wanted electricity in my house; it seemed unnecessary because, as I had explained to a friend, "I have a headlamp to see which part of me is standing in which part of the house." In my estimation, there are far too many lights in the world; streetlights, car lights, tiny lights in the glove box; front and back porch lights, lights in the ceiling, under the cabinets, and in the refrigerator; lights working their way across undulating surfaces, so you could guess the couch cushions are soft and the bathroom sink will bruise your hip if you totter into it in the middle of the night.

I wondered if all that light was somehow causing us to forget things, blinding us to the truth that a little darkness can be a good thing. When I was in the hospital, lights were on all the time, day or night—lights from the heart monitor, the automatic blood pressure cuff, the nurses' station. And then there were all the electronically induced noises: beeps and hums, and *pssst*-ing sounds from the oxygen generator. There were noises from my roommate; she was uncomfortable, but there was nothing I could do. I just lay there, hoping the noise would dampen, spread itself into the mattresses and the cotton blankets that they'd sometimes warm for us in a microwave oven. I wished for more silence, and then once she had passed, wanted more noise. I'm fickle like that.

But I was certain I wanted my little house to be as quiet as possible, to bypass the racket created by a humming refrigerator and a buzzing fluorescent light. I wanted a chance to hear myself breathe, and to notice that my inhalations jibe with RooDee's and my heartbeat is making the sheet rustle. As a result, I decided to install a mere smidgen of electricity so I could cut carrots early in the morning without losing a finger and avoid putting my shirt on inside out (something I've done plenty of times with or without a lightbulb).

I ended up with fifty feet of copper wire stringing four wall outlets and a couple of overhead lights together, and then connected that to one of the most expensive and mystical contraptions ever: a 240-watt solar electric system. It's a small system ("more of a suggestion than the real deal," one guy had joked when he compared my system to the "normal one down the street") but still an impressive-looking setup, like part of a NASA space shuttle had landed next to my house, which made me feel that something intelligent was going on in the backyard.

To this day, I have no idea how the thing works—something about how the sun frees the electrons in the silicon panels, not by warming them but by simply shining on them, which made me wonder if I should install a mirror next to the panels to generate even more electricity, or place them in water to enlarge the sunrays like how my legs look bigger when I soak them in a swimming pool. These two ideas make me wonder if I've just proven that I don't know the first thing about solar electricity.

Over time, I've gotten comfortable with my limited understanding of what is actually happening with the system. All I needed to know was that no electricity could be generated at night, less electricity could be generated in the long dark winter, and if I tried to run an electric coffeemaker, everything would shut down (the system couldn't supply the 1,200 watts of electricity needed to heat up the water). All of a sudden, I had to pay attention to what I was plugging in and for how long, and I also had to make sure everything with the solar electric system stayed in good condition. *Nothing* could ever go wrong with the magical panels, battery, inverter, or meter—nothing ever!—or I'd have to live with the consequences of getting dressed in the dark: one black sock and one white, which would seem to beam like a spotlight when I crossed my legs in a meeting.

Lightning struck again—blue-white light spun RooDee around in a tight circle, and then she began pacing from one end of the mattress to the other.

"Shit!" I shouted over the roar of wind in the eaves.

I stared at my dog for a minute, trying to decide what to do, and then suddenly shoved the blankets off and huffed down the ladder. A minute later, wearing my rain gear and a head-lamp, I shimmied back up the ladder to help RooDee down to the living room, where she immediately started panting and shaking.

"Stay put," I offered (like she had any choice), and then I stepped into the storm and closed the door behind me. The backyard was a lake, pooled up from my house to the foundation of Rita's house. I stuck my feet in my boots and launched myself off the porch into the rain, running as fast as I could to Hugh and Annie's garage for a wrench.

Years ago, I met a guy who had been electrocuted in his house while talking on the phone. He had been talking with his brother when lightning struck the house and traveled through the wiring, including the phone line, directly into his left ear. The jolt melted his ear and the phone receiver, and blew him backward across his kitchen. He tore the phone off the wall when he got tossed, landing on his back in his living room. The electric current entered his head and followed the lines of his vasculature, from his cranial fluid down his spinal cord, along veins, arteries, and capillaries to terminate at his left foot, where it melted the heel off his shoe. He woke up three days later in the hospital with third-degree burns and an electrical problem with his heart—a problem similar enough to mine that he also had an implanted defibrillator, which then gave us a chance to bond in the waiting room at the doctor's office.

Somewhere in the mix of discovering we both had defibrillators, he told me about his accident and turned his head so I could see his ear was missing. "Wow, I hadn't even noticed that," I lied. And then he shyly let me know that my shirt was on inside out.

I was thinking about that guy as I ran from my house to the garage, wondering if all the fillings in my head, the buttons on my raincoat, or the eyelets on my boots were acting like small lightning rods. I grabbed a wrench out of the garage and headed back to the little house to reconnect the grounding wire.

When I got back, another bolt of lightning hit; this time it was closer and turned the low clouds a strange blue-white. I stretched the cable from the grounding rod near the fence back over to the house. All the while, the hood of my jacket kept getting caught up in the wind, twisting into the headlamp so I was in the dark. I kneeled next to the house and ripped the hood back, letting the rain soak my head, pelting my scalp like sand thrown through a box fan.

Ten minutes went by as I tried to unscrew the wire nut that pigtailed out of my house. It was a stubby little green wire, maybe two inches long, that terminated in a copper fitting and a nut; "stylishly hidden," I had once boasted as I showed off the way the connection was tucked behind the wheel well and under the house.

"What a complete pain in the ass," I shouted in frustration.

The wrench kept getting jammed up against the trailer, and my wrists suddenly seemed to bend at all the wrong angles. Meanwhile, the rain had changed direction, causing me to shut my eyes and bow my head farther into my chest, shoving my shoulders up to my ears for protection. It was a praying posture, fitting for the situation.

My fingers were working blind: finding the nut with the left hand, twisting the wrench with the right. Scraping the knuckles on the siding, losing the nut, finding the nut . . . and so on. At one point, I heard myself making tiny mewing sounds, audible over the storm, and then there was a roaring electrical growl just before a massive *kaboom!*

"Ack!" I yelled.

It wasn't lightning. The transformer posted on the telephone pole in front of Rita's house had just exploded like a bomb blast. I spun out of my kneeling position and landed on my butt, right hand still clutching the wrench, left hand landing in the garden mud.

"Ack!" I yelled again, dazed, and then I started to laugh. I realized I hadn't been seeing lightning at all; it had been transformers blowing up all over town, wires crackling and shorting out as they were blown by the storm into tree branches.

I noticed that my house was likely the only house lit up in the neighborhood, the only surviving source of electricity in a multiblock radius. I lay faceup in the yard, letting the rain continue to drench me. It smelled suddenly sweet, like rain and mud and no worries.

"Oh my God," I said to my dog, snickering as I walked in the house a few minutes later. "That was epic! Ridiculous. Let me tell ya what just happened."

I like that my day-to-day invites a bit of monkey business with nature. Sometimes it's a big deal like a rainstorm, and other times it's something random like the day a squirrel launched itself off the fence practically into my arms (my theory is that it thought I was a short tree). Perplexed and a little frightened, I ran across the yard and locked myself in Rita's house; maybe I didn't want to be a friend to the woodland creatures (my childhood dream) after all. Another time, I followed a line of ants swarming the edge of the sidewalk—an ant superhighway that went on for two blocks and ended with a cluster of ants carrying a Cheeto on their backs. It was surreal, and I took a picture of it to prove it happened.

Most of my interactions with nature are accidental collisions, like when I have to race from my house to Rita's tap early in the morning to fill my water jug. I usually dash out wearing nothing but my underwear and a raincoat, grumbling at myself for failing to install a crazy little thing called "indoor plumbing"; I grouse and whine, and notice it really *is* raining hard enough to sting and that the grass has gotten so saturated it feels like a sponge cake. I might see that my new raincoat is perfect except for the fact that it doesn't cover and the hood flops in my face, or I might notice that it's not nearly as cold as it was yesterday, that spring has arrived, which makes me skip back to the little house.

I don't remember noticing the subtle shift toward spring when I lived in my big house; maybe because I was so preoccupied with other things, or maybe it was simple proximity. Spring now launches itself like a space shuttle mission inches from my head, and so graphically I can practically hear the "Three-two-one, GO, GO, GO!" as the sun peeks over the garage.

Sometimes I worry that I'll slide back into the mindless rotisserie of work and projects that guided me in my old house; I'll fixate on one pimple in my life or get so accustomed to the way things work in the backyard—like seeing the rain grow into a lake in front of my house (as it always does in winter), that I'll grow numb to the way nature can leave me awestruck. I worry that I'll fall asleep at the switch, only to wake up years later and find that I can't remember what I did last week or the month before that, nor do I recognize the old lady staring back at me in the mirror.

That said, as I've gotten older, I've found that I crave a certain predictability in each day; my alarm will ring at just the right moment, my truck will start precisely like it did the day before, and I'll drive to the office without incident, where I'll tap away at my computer just like always, like I'm supposed to and want to, and hope to do tomorrow. I'll return home and walk the dog, make a bit of dinner, chat with Rita, read a book, or watch an episode of *Glee*. Each day will present itself and end with a string of predictable events, safe and tidy, where I can float through life as the planet rotates (again) from winter into spring, and the only rebellious thing I'll do for months is decide not to get a flu shot.

Therein lies the challenge: The trees don't bud out of habit, and I don't want to sleep through my life, which is why I appreciate my less-than-convenient conveniences—a compost toilet, a water jug filled up at Rita's spigot, and 240 watts of electricity generated out of solar panels that I don't understand. Whatever you call them, my systems keep me plugged into the day in a unique way. They keep me sober, and that's a good thing.

Most of the time, I appreciate the way my house is set up,

but I still sometimes miss my shower. In my old house, it was my favorite place to think, and now, when I shower at work or at Rita's, I seem more focused on getting things done as quickly as possible.

When I first arrived in the backyard, my friends would invite me over for dinner and a shower. I'd shower at Jenn and Kellie's house, Hugh and Annie's, Candyce and Paula's, Justin's, Liz's, Jennifer's, Mike's, or Steve's. Showering at work was also an easy solution; I had to go to work anyway, so why not go in early and take advantage of their hot water? The downside was that the shower looked and smelled just like the locker rooms of my youth, when I was forced to dress for gym or suit up for track practice amid twenty or thirty other girls who were just as self-conscious as me. That was thirty years ago, but the same self-conscious insecurity flared when I walked into the locker room at work for the first time. Fortunately, I'd planned right and arrived a half hour before the bike commuters arrived.

I stripped naked and placed all my clothes in an empty, open locker, wrapped myself in a towel, and donned my shower slippers. I slammed the locker closed and turned toward the showers, when I realized I'd just shut my clothes in a padlocked cabinet.

The lockers had a combination lock fixed to the front of the unit. When you signed up as a bike commuter, you were assigned a locker along with a secret combination. Apparently, the locker I'd found open was an accident, and I was left standing there in a towel, feeling my chest sink just like it did in eighth grade. I sat down on a bench and tried to think. I mulled over a couple of options, including crawling through the ventilation system to my car.

I waited in my towel for about thirty minutes, occasionally spinning random numbers into the combination lock, hoping to get lucky, until the first biker arrived. I tried not to lunge at her when she walked in, and instead smiled. "Oh, hey," I said, "I seem to have locked my clothes in this locker." I played it off as nonchalant, like I walked around naked in the locker room all the time. She went into the hall and called Building Services, and laughed when I thanked her and explained that I had been thinking about tossing a flip-flop out the door with a note reading: "NAKED. SEND HELP!"

After that experience, I started showering at work only if absolutely necessary and instead showered fairly regularly at Rita's house. It was less problematic, except for the occasional need to race across the backyard wearing nothing but a towel, and it became a habit—a routine that involved me checking in with Rita even though I knew, over time, that she didn't give a hoot. But it was our way of living together, and my way of letting her know how much I appreciated her generosity. It went like this:

Me: "Rita, can I take a shower?"

Rita: "Yes. I don't know why you keep asking."

Me: "I like to ask."

Rita: "Hummm," she'd mutter as she poked her nose back into her book.

And then when I would pop out of the bathroom fifteen minutes later, I'd chirp: "Who's clean?" As I walked across her living room, wearing nothing but a towel, ready to launch myself nearly naked across the backyard and into my house.

Rita: "Jesus, Mary, and Joseph! I forgot you were here."

Me: "That was the best shower ever! In a thousand million years of people bathing and showering, that was the best!"

Rita: "Hummm," she would say as she poked her nose back into her book.

So it started, and then continued for years.

Slack Line

There are seven Internet signals that radiate through the walls of my little house, squeezing into the living room, kitchen, and sleeping loft. I can't access any of them because they require a password, so I trek over to Hugh and Annie's house and ask them to plug a little forklike antenna into the Internet box that sits under their computer. Once the fork is in place and my laptop properly positioned, I can use the Internet to answer all my most important questions, like how many times does the human heart beat each day (about 100,000), is there really an island where everyone has six fingers on each hand (no), what is the average square footage of a home in America (2,349) versus the UK (815). After doing this vital research, I might watch a few videos of sleeping kittens and puppies, sitting there dumbfounded, sighing and laughing, until I remember that I came over and had Hugh plug the fork into the box because I wanted to research how to take Rita's kitchen faucet apart and replace the gaskets to make it stop dripping. So I watch three videos of a guy taking a faucet apart, and a fourth showing the same guy explaining how to fish small screws out of the drain after you've accidentally dropped them while fixing the faucet.

I could spend hours doing this sort of thing, hopping from one video or fascinating bit of information to another, until suddenly I get a cramp in my calf or my eyes feel gritty, and I realize I've spent the past two hours hovering over my computer with my back curled like a question mark. Given that—my weak mind and my ability to follow the shiny ball of more and more and more information—it's probably best that there's no Internet connection in my house.

Sometimes I wonder what we'd all be doing if we weren't spending so much time hovering over our electronic gadgets, watching videos, playing games, confirming that our eyes do not fog up in the shower because they are warm and salty (a fact that I recently looked up on the Internet). Here's what I have to remind myself of, what I have to tell myself when I'm pining to quickly grab a computer to see what time the sun rises in the morning: The Internet is dumb.

The Internet, with all its access to brain research, anthropology journals, social studies networks, and biographies and autobiographies, can't begin to map the complexity of our lives, or how we each affect others. Last week, a guy made my day by telling me he couldn't believe I was forty-nine years old. Bless his soul.

Similarly, despite all its millions of data points and access to academic journals, Animal Planet, and thousands of short videos showing pets doing funny things, the Internet can't begin to articulate the confusion that comes with nature, how it is both stunning and brutal.

A few years ago, I stepped out of my little house, reveling in the way the sky was so blue it looked fake, like a filtered photo doctored to make you feel an immense sense of optimism—and then, a few minutes later, a bit of horror. I found a cathead near my truck. It was just the head, lying there like a tennis ball. No arms or legs or tail or collar with a name tag. There was no explanation other than a guess that maybe a raccoon or a fox had gotten to it. It made me scream and then nearly cry, and then I put it in a shoe box and buried it in the woods. I would never have the courage to go looking for something so gruesome, although I still can't explain why all these years later I still study "Cat Missing" signs posted on telephone poles or at the co-op, wondering if someone is missing the cat (head) I put in the shoe box.

Nature is confounding in the way it pulls us apart and then puts us back together again. If you Google "cathead," all you'll find is references to ships and large hats.

All that said, I'm a total sucker for Netflix, a website where you can watch movies and television shows instantly on your computer. I try not to mention this fetish or any of my absent-minded dillydallying when people ask how I spend my free time now that I'm not working as much. Instead, I might mention that I recently helped someone tear down an old garage, and that I've been volunteering at the Salvation Army soup kitchen; and then I'll talk about my other amazing volunteer activities like installing grip bars along the kitchen counter at Rita's house. And all of that is true: I enjoy pitching in on various projects and hope that I'm being helpful, but I also spend an awful lot of time goofing off.

I spent almost an hour trying to recondition an oscillating fan that I found in a junk pile. I'm not certain, but I think it was tossed out because it had a frightening wad of human hair wrapped around the spindle where the fan blades connect to the motor. It was disgusting and curious, and exactly the sort of thing you find on junk day in Olympia.

I love junk day. Everyone puts out their rubbish—their busted-up washing machines and hot water heaters, dysfunctional blenders and vacuum cleaners—so everything can be hauled off to the dump. But before they go, passersby like me can walk around scanning for useful goods, occasionally lunging into the debris piles like pearl divers. Last year, I found a perfectly good electric lawn mower that I was able to rewire and repair with a couple rolls of duct tape; today I found this hairy fan.

I took everything apart in the garage, cut the toupee out of the machinery, and repaired a break in the electric cord. I sprayed the fan with vinegar and swabbed the plastic, dabbing here and there, and flipping the unit like it was a newborn and I was a neonatal surgeon.

I have a keen respect for fans. I grew up in the Midwest, where the summer heat can turn your car seat into a waffle iron, where people stroke out from sun poisoning and everyone owns a box fan even if they have air-conditioning. On hot days, my friend Chinn and I would pedal over to the 7-Eleven, where we'd sneak into the walk-in cooler and sit around on the beer cases until we shivered. At night, my siblings and I would fall asleep on top of our covers, listening to the chatter of a box fan drowning out the whip-poor-wills and cicadas, my father's snoring, and the ten-o'clock news saying it would be just as hot tomorrow.

In the Pacific Northwest, fans are an afterthought. They move moisture and odors, and only serve to cool things down when you're doing something weird like canning beans or drying fruit, or running your stove to full capacity in the middle of the summer. So it doesn't surprise me that I'd find a perfectly good fan among a pile of old curled-up shoes and stained T-shirts. People here don't understand how a fan can save your life.

Usually, I'll fix something and set it on a shelf in the garage, where it will sit, orphaned next to the half-empty paint cans and bicycle parts, until a few weeks later, when I'll open the door and realize I don't really need a light-up Santa, so I'll take it to Goodwill or walk it over to the "Free" box near the food co-op, where I'll have a moment of anxiety wondering if I really should keep the item because maybe, someday, I'll decide I really *do* want a festive Santa, no matter how disfigured.

I'm telling you this because I've found that even when you have your freedom—when you've liberated yourself from your debt, and are happy enough living like a polar bear in winter— even then, you're still stuck with who you are.

Fortunately, I'm also stuck with awesome friends.

Earlier today, out of the blue, Hugh and Annie's daughter, Keeva, set up a slack line (a flat strap similar to a tightrope wire but wider and friendlier) between her house and mine, and proceeded to walk heel to toe across the backyard without ever stepping foot on the grass. She was so good at this particular task that I decided to put a garden sprinkler in her path, wondering if she could maneuver past the wet strap even with water spraying up into her eyes like a blindfold, but she defied the odds and performed like a champion, and then gave me several lessons for bounding up on the line and taking a few steps. We were about to take things to a whole new level, whistling while we walked or juggling knives and chain saws, when we noticed that the anchoring post closest to Hugh and Annie's house was starting to cleave forward. We both screamed and seemed to run in slow motion toward the post, laughing when we got there, and then quickly dismantled the contraption be-fore either of us landed on our ear as the carport post dove forward into the backyard, quickly followed by the entire roof structure.

Years ago, when I met Hugh and Annie, I never would have guessed that they would become two of my closest friends, let alone that their daughter would grow up before my eyes and turn into someone who would know how to engineer a slack line.

///////////////////

When I first moved into the backyard, there weren't any Inter-net signals infiltrating my house, and Hugh and Annie didn't have the box with its fork accessory; instead, they had a thick cable that connected their computer to their phone line, which then connected to some massive tower that seemed to fail every week or so as it struggled to keep up with everyone's desire to check their e-mail. Back then (in "ye old days," eight years ago), if we wanted to watch a video we'd huddle together in their living room and watch a movie through a DVD player attached to a very small portable television, or we'd cram together around their kitchen table and watch something on their computer that sat on an adjacent desk. The whole experience was very similar to how people used to listen to the radio, where they'd gather up and some would knit or whittle while others would lean on their elbows and daydream themselves into whatever story was being told at the moment.

In "ye old days," we would occasionally pull the television and DVD player outside onto Rita's patio, so we could watch a movie or an episode of *Gilmore Girls* while Rita got ready for bed. At those times, everything in the backyard seemed to pull together—the trees and bushes, the garage and the smell of raw, freshly turned dirt in the garden would step forward, lean in, and watch the movie with us. Cinema night on the patio was always a highlight for me.

Game night was equally awesome.

Occasionally, we'd have an impromptu steely-eyed game of Clue, where each of us would collect information like a detective as we moved our little pieces around the board, trying to determine who killed the subject with what weapon in what room. It was very challenging, and as a state investigator, I found myself personally challenged to be at my best, which most often looked like me sitting there with a squishy look on my face while Hugh, Annie, Keeva, and Kellen took copious notes.

"Hummm," they would mutter as, heads down, they would scribble something into their notepads to describe my latest play in the game.

It was a level of intellectual competition I'd never experienced before, and I found myself feeling the need to cheat, to suddenly break everyone's concentration by declaring a "tea break," when I'd wander off to the kitchen to make a snack before Kellen (only nine, then ten, then thirteen years old) could beat me.

The last time we played Clue was in the middle of a snowstorm, huddled in Rita's house, which was slowly dropping in temperature because the power was out. Hugh, Annie, Keeva, Kellen, and I sat around the game board with our headlamps, holding our cards and trying to navigate our playing pieces, while Rita sat nearby, bundled in a stocking cap, a down coat, and two blankets. It was 69 degrees in her house. A heat wave compared with mine, but Rita sat in her arctic outerwear. She nearly froze to death as we sat around in light sweaters, enjoying the 67-degree then 62-degree temperatures while taking notes (or not). It was a bit sad when the electricity came back on; we all liked the ad-libbed slumber party that was developing in Rita's living room.

At holidays and birthdays, we'd coordinate our schedules for dinner and gift-giving. A few months after I moved into the backyard, I started shopping for Rita, wandering back and forth down the aisles, looking for everything on her list: the largest, most obnoxiously massive box of Rice Krispies ever produced, frozen mac and cheese, Kleenex, milk. Everything was very specific; I wasn't supposed to get any sort of toilet paper but the Charmin "mega soft," and I couldn't just get the denture powder on sale but only the Top Care brand of tablets. It was awkward at first, making me eye-roll when Rita would bristle at my choice of an alternative brand of frozen lasagna, but then, over time, I realized I too was extra-picky about what type of bread I ate, the kind of toothpaste, coffee, half-and-half, and beer I wanted—it was all very personal and, depending on the item, brought varying degrees of excited anticipation, which registered by me humming or whistling while I unloaded groceries, sticking the perishables in my blue ice chest, the canned goods above the dinner dishes, and the dry goods in the drawer to the left of the kitchen sink.

On occasion, I became Rita's chauffeur, taking her to Kellen's baseball games, to graduation ceremonies, her hairdresser's wedding, and the occasional doctor's appointment. I liked doing this stuff, parking in a restricted space close to the front door of the optometrist's office, unloading the wheelchair, helping Rita stand and then shuffle into the chair. I liked learning how to buckle her into the car seat, reaching across her the way I used to do with my four-year-old niece, and coming to understand the physics of supporting her as she teetered forward out of the car from a seated position to standing, trying to perfect the subtle art of providing dignity and grace in a moment of awkwardness.

Similarly, Hugh and Annie became my advocates, taking me to the emergency room or to the hospital when I had surgery. I'll never forget Annie sitting with me after I'd had a heart procedure that hadn't gone so well. The doctor had tried to use a laser to burn away a bit of the interior of my heart's left ventricle, flash-frying it so it wouldn't conduct an electrical current that would in turn reduce the number of extra, misfired heartbeats. It hadn't gone as planned, and he had given up before placing me in any greater harm; and I had started crying when I learned that nothing had changed. My heart was still broken, and *that* broke my heart even more. I curled into a small ball in my hospital bed as Annie sat with me, crying nearly as much as me. After a few minutes, she asked if I wanted to see how she sometimes handled her disappointment.

"Ya," I answered, thinking she'd pick up the nearby bowl of Jell-O and jab it with a fork.

Instead, she stood up, closed her eyes, and started tap-dancing. She had studied dancing in New York, and she knew what she was doing, stuttering her feet and keeping her arms near her sides, tense, like she was reliving a moment when she'd been caught up short by a grade-school bully. She danced in one spot like that for a minute or so, moving her feet so methodically I could feel the heel strikes and toe-taps pass across the hospital floor into the bed, the mattress, my body, my toes. I could feel what she felt, and then her body changed. Her feet moved even faster and kicked higher, and her chest expanded so she could windmill her arms as she slowly turned in a circle, tapping away until a smile peeked out below her closed eyes, and then a bigger smile, like a balloon lifting off the floor, bigger and bigger until she threw open her eyes and excitedly looked at me, spun around, and closed with a loud "Ta-daaaa!"

It was so fantastic, it made me laugh even as I lay there disoriented and confused.

///////////////////

There were a lot of logistical questions when I first moved into the backyard: Where should I set the house, park my car, get mail, and stash my ever-changing array of "found" items: wood scraps, a light-up Santa, and other riprap that seemed to easily float in and out of the garage? These things were easy to sort out, like figuring out how to engineer a little house to drag it down the highway. You sort through the options, collaborate, and make a decision.

Other issues were more nuanced, and even though I don't want to beat you up with my comparisons, those sticky wickets were very similar to learning that a rafter tail will split if you don't drill a hole before screwing it into the wall. Some things you learn through trial and error, or by repeatedly using your body until it grows its own muscle memory and no longer needs your brainy guidance to know how best to hold a nail gun.

When I first moved into the backyard, I was completely flummoxed by which was better: knocking and then opening Rita's door with the house key she had given me, or knocking and waiting for her to rise out of her chair like an old ship being raised from the deep dark sea. She'd eventually get to a standing position, steady herself, and then reach for her tripod cane to begin the process of walking around the kitchen table to the front door—a journey no less epic than rounding Cape Horn. Meanwhile, I would stand on the other side of the door, worrying that I shouldn't have bothered her in the first place.

It became easier to knock, pause for a second, and then walk in saying, "Candy Gram!" I still do that, all these years later, whether Rita is listening or not.

We discovered how to keep the peace: how I shouldn't draw water from Rita's tap before eight in the morning because the pipes would hum and wake her up, and how RooDee shouldn't be out at four in the afternoon because, apparently, she liked to scare the mailman by behaving as if she wanted to rip the logo off his letter bag, shirt, hat, and back pants pocket.

Hugh, Annie, Rita, and I saw each other nearly every day, but it didn't feel like my house was an extension of theirs, like an outdoor bedroom or apartment. I was autonomous—a close neighbor, who also took showers at Rita's, stored ice cream in her freezer, and watched *Wheel of Fortune* with her. Somehow we all found our place, and figured out how to share what we had.

Just now, writing this, it sounds lovely (and it has been), but there have been weird moments. One time, when Kellen was about eight years old, I took him to baseball practice and ended up lounging around on the grass with him and his baseball buddies, waiting for the coach to show up. We were shooting the shit about how fast we could run if we had giant Slinkys strapped to our shoes, when one of the boys suddenly looked at me and suspiciously asked if I was Kellen's aunt.

"Well, no," I said calmly, smiling. "I just live in the backyard."

He pondered this for a minute and then belted out in shock, "Oh my God, you're one of the homeless people!" He said it innocently and emphatically.

Kellen and I simultaneously went to bat with explanations. "She has a house in the corner," he said.

"It's really cute and nice," I offered, using a schoolteacher tone, "and I live there with a Keebler Elf and several small woodland creatures. It's actually quite lovely . . . well, except for the squirrels. They have terrible gas—perhaps a dietary issue. Their nuts give them gas."

The kids looked at me for a minute, and then all of us burst into laughter. I drove home later, pondering the kid's comment about my being homeless. It stung, and made me feel that I needed to explain something about myself, like living in the backyard was a bad thing. But it didn't feel that way, and in fact felt like one of the best living arrangements I'd ever had.

In all these years, there haven't been lingering hard feelings: no big arguments brewing, no power plays or hierarchy that need shuffling every once in a while. Instead, we all get along incredibly well for close-quartered neighbors, with the occasional disagreement about minor things.

This is what Rita and I argued about: the sweetness of cinnamon (I know, a very big issue indeed). I swore cinnamon was savory not sweet, and Rita swore she knew better. I'll never forget storming out of her house, seriously offended by her getting in the way of my baking, as an apple pie dotted with sugar and cinnamon baked away in her oven. She had screeched "Ack, ack, ack" like I was sprinkling acid on the pie, like she was personally being injured by my cinnamon. It bugged the shit out of me. It was my pie, and she didn't get to say shit about it!

"Man-o-man," I had said later, "you really pissed me off." And then Rita had said, "Oh. Hummm. Yes, I can see that."

As it turns out, we were both right. A few days after the argument, I looked up cinnamon on the Internet and discovered that it's both sweet and savory; it can go either way. And for years, we'd tease each other, saying, "Oh my, don't want a repeat of the cinnamon incident," when we'd feel ourselves on the verge of an argument.

Most arguments look ridiculous when you put them on paper; this one is no different.

///////////////////

Over time, Home became something defined as much by my house as by the way Rita would call me at six o'clock to see if I wanted to watch the news; by how every December, a Christmas tree would arrive on the top of Hugh and Annie's small car, picked and pruned by Keeva and Kellen, and then be set up in their living room like a giant schnoz on the face of a small man. Home became the place I most wanted to be when I was feeling good or bad, busy or lazy, confused or clearheaded. Home was where Rita lived; it was Hugh and Annie's house, the carport, the driveway, the fir tree, the garbage bins, the wind that came out of the south and smashed into my house, and the smell of cedar that still wafts out of my loft even after almost a decade.

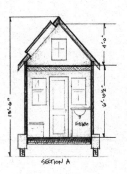

15'-6"

4'-0"

6'-10½"

KITCHEN

SECTION A

Nearly All My Stuff ~~Except~~ Some I can't Remember! 305½

Household Stuff	Personal Stuff		FUN STUFF	Automotive + Tools
2 Water Jugs	Winter Hat	Pajama Bottoms	2 Maps	Honda
Cigar Box	Sun Hat	2 Pair Eye Glasses	Gazateer	Small Doll
Cutting Board	½ Scarf franken	Sunglasses	Backpack	Small Bead
Tea Kettle	Full Scarf	2 Necklaces	Therma Rest	2 Sweet Grass
Hippo Match Hold	Yoga Pants	1 Ring	Old Tent	Glove Box full of Crap
Salt + Pepper Pigs	Puffy Coat	1 Bracelett	Vase w/ wheat	
Thermos	Down Coat	Down Booties	2 Old Coins	
3 Coffee Cups	John's Coat	Gaiters	Grrr Dish	Chop Saw
2 Plates	Fleece Coat	Over Mitts	Window Elf	Table Saw
2 Bowls	Sweater	3 Pair Earrings	Tray of Shells	Jig Saw
John's Mug	Mittens	Broken Watch	Prayer Box	Saws All
5 Spoons	2 Thermal Shirts	Mud Boots	2 Buddha Art	Cive Saw
4 Forks	2 Long Johns	Climbing Shoes	2 Framed Photos	Nail Gun
1 Spork	Tough Rain Coat	Harness + Rack	2 Post Cards	Compresser
2 Pair Chopsticks	Rain Pants	2 Slings	23 Books	Palm Sand
Can Opener	Rain Bibs	Rings (Pull up)	10 Journals	Planer
Cut down Wood Spoon	3 Blouses	Sleeping Bag	20 CD/DVDs	Skillsaw
Cut down Spatula	2 Jeans	Stuff Sack	Drafting Arm + Tools	Protective Stuff
Fry Pan	Fancy Pants	Camp Stove + Pots	Laptop + charger	Bucket of Hand Tools
Serving Tray	3 T-Shirts	Towel	Cell Phone + charger	3 X-Tension cords
Toast Thing	Swim Suit	Head Lamp	Ear Phones	
2 Cook Pots also used for Camping	2 Pairs Socks	Water Filter	7 Flash Drives	
Coffee Filter	2 Panties	Pocket Knife - Used in Kitchen	At Work:	
Jar of rice	3 Bras	Ice Axe - Not Used in Kitchen	Globe	2 Old Defibrillators
Jar of Cluck Cluck food	Coveralls	Hiking Poles	Bird Clock	3 Books
Fire extinguisher	Black Pumps	Kayak + Paddles	Photo's + Shells	Towel
Cigar Box	Loafers	Dry Bag	A dried up Gecko	Flip Flops
3 dish towels	2 Flip Flops	Pump + Rope	Turtle Shell	
	Running Shoes		Awards	

KITCHEN!, KITCHEN, KITCHEN !!, CLOTHES, FUN STUFF, TOOLS + CAR

				More Tools:
3 Bed Sheets	2 Oil Lamps	Metal Bucket	Arbor	3 Clamps
7 Quilts	2 Step Stools	Tiki Totem Pole	Clippers	Lamp
2 Bath Towels	1 Jar Q-Tips	Budha + Bench	Bamboo in a Pot	Battery Charger
3 Couch Pillows	Wool Mattress	Wind Chime	3 Flower Pots	Cordless Drill
2 Bed Pillows	Mem. Foam	Buster the Pig	2 Porch Lamps	Impact Driver
Basket of Vitamins, Boo Boo Dust, Bathroom Things	Flashlight	Welcome Mat	Candle Holder	Scrapers
	2 Wash Cloths	Stained Glass Window	Rocking Chair	Box w/ Glue Plugs Screws

BED/BATH, GARDEN STUFF, Tools

ROODEE'S STUFF: 2 Covers, Bed, Water/Food Dish, 2 Collars, Leash, 7 Food Bins, 2 Brushes seldom used

A Six-Inch Drop Hitch

Currently, I keep my camping knife in the drawer near the stove; it sits there with five other pieces of silverware, an oven mitt, a spatula, a can opener, and a box of matches. Nearby I keep three coffee cups, a couple of plates, and a tin of birdseed; there's also a decorative sugar bowl shaped like a monkey head, and a platelike toaster with little arms that rise up to hold bread over an open flame. Everything has a purpose or tells a story (or both), like the way I got the toaster as a birthday present from a friend and was so excited to use it that I immediately plopped it on the stove with two slices of bread, blabbing about how this was the best present ever and, my God, this is genius, while my friend sat on the couch and smiled very big. I continued to flip the hot bread for twenty minutes, waiting for it to turn brown, but all it did was melt part of the twisty knob for my stove and curl the bread like an old shoe. This compelled my friend to bang his "toast" on the countertop, denting it, which threw us into hysterics. I'm saving the toaster to give it back to him in a few years, when he needs a little lift in his day and wants to remember how funny it is to fake-bite bread and pretend your teeth have broken.

It's weird to take stock of what you keep and what you let go of. I recently counted and categorized all my stuff, and discovered that I have 305 things, ranging from my toothbrush and silverware to my truck and all the crap that seems to have accumulated in the glove box. The list invited all sorts of contemplative high jinks, where I sincerely marveled over the brilliance of my multitool pocketknife and the way I could use the scissors, or open a bottle, cut cheese, or even break out of prison with it. I puzzled over why we say "pants" instead of "pant," and whether I got to count sock pairs (clearly two items) as a single thing. I wondered why I still held on to my pig-shaped pepper shaker after he had fallen off the counter and shattered into a dozen irreconcilable pieces. I had glued him back together the best I could, and he leaned lumpily next to his pig-shaped partner, the saltshaker.

I found myself staring at the list and wondering what Sherlock Holmes would deduce about the person who owned all this stuff. Occupation, hobbies, gender? I suddenly felt incredibly self-conscious, recognizing that if I made a pie chart of possessions, most of the pie would be filled with burly things: jigsaws, camping gear, unsexy long johns, and the like; and one small sliver would be dedicated to what some people would call normal lady things (panties, bras, a dress, a skirt, two necklaces, seven ponytail holders). What kind of woman was I, and what would others say if they knew the last gadget I bought (a spontaneous purchase) was a six-inch drop hitch, a heavy slug of metal designed to connect a trailer to a truck?

My point in all of this is that a little self-awareness can lead to a lot of self-conscious prattling, which is a perfect springboard for tossing the list aside and going for a walk.

A few years ago, my mom and I were talking about how we either keep or let go of things, and agreed that she was more of a "hanger-on-er" than me. This discussion came up after an argument about me giving away a camera that she had given me, and how could I let go of things so casually? The camera was a Nikon, a fancy professional deal that had been my grandfather's, one he had picked up in Japan, and it had passed along to my mom when he died. My mom had gifted it to me, and later I had gifted it to my sixteen-year-old niece. And in the end, my mom felt I'd betrayed her in the deepest way possible . . . like I'd given up on her and not the camera.

My mom saw me as cavalier and reckless, a compulsive "let-er-goer" in our conversation and I viewed her as a neurotic hoarder. How else could I explain the way my mom has shelves full of pinch pots, crayon drawings, and odd little knickknacks that my siblings and I created in grade school? As I talked to her on the phone, I could imagine her basement, full of boxes: old report cards, newspaper clippings, wedding announcements, and blurry photos showing my dad holding me as a baby, pulling cake out of my brother's hair when he was a toddler, smiling at my sister minutes after her first baby was born, and standing awkwardly beside me with my car loaded to the gills the day I left the Midwest and moved to Olympia. Who else but a hoarder would hang on to the stuffed animal that her mother once gave her, to her father's spectacles and his Bible, to scrapbooks filled with photos of relatives no one remembers.

Regardless of how I wish it weren't true, my mom was right in our argument: I had regifted her camera and felt fine about it. I was a let-er-goer and she was a hanger-on-er, but that doesn't mean I don't lean into her territory every once in a while.

Among the extremely useful things I store in my house is a six-inch neck scarf, a gift from Kellen—something he had promised me in a Christmas card, written in his classic seven-year-old print: "I love you. I well give you a scarf." Months later, he walked up to me and out of the blue threw a piece of orange knitting at me (a short, thin piece, like a special key fob). "I got tired," he offered.

I'm holding on to the scarf so I can wear it to his future college graduation, or some other event that honors Kellen Hugh MacNally, where I can be the strange lady in the back row with an orange key fob safety-pinned to her blouse. And if ever asked to propose a toast, I can stand proud, holding my tie/key fob and explain how he had saved my sense of well-being the day he told his friend I wasn't homeless.

So I've held on to Kellen's scarf and a small window elf that was felted by a friend's four-year-old. I have a box of seashells, a silver dollar, and a buffalo nickel. I have one of my dog's baby teeth, a clay button that goes to the first sweater that my friend Beth knitted, and a pair of climbing shoes that are held together with duct tape. Those shoes remind me of who I used to be; how I'd gladly load into a car at ten o'clock at night, heading out to the crags with my friends, where we'd drive half the night and then sleep for a few hours at the trailhead, like kittens, in the back of the car. We'd push ourselves through the day, sweating and grunting, and hanging by our knuckles as we attempted overly ambitious, nasty climbs called something inane like "Kiss of the Crowbar." I was strong and eager, and willing to drag myself (and my shoes) on any number of epic weekend adventures.

Now I am less eager, and like it or not, I mostly wear my climbing shoes when I walk up the ladder to clean the neighbor's gutters. But there's some psychology involved; I find myself braver and younger when I'm cleaning the roof.

I haven't done much redecorating over the years. I have the same bamboo blinds and the same wool rug that collects dog hair like it's spun out of Scotch tape, the same pillows, and the same wicker basket full of camping gear, down booties (a winter necessity), and Kellen's six-inch neck scarf. I've held on to a few mementos, but much more has come and gone. I've ushered in new jeans, T-shirts, coveralls, dish towels, eyeglasses, a pair of pumps, some underwear, tennis shoes, flip-flops, socks, a bath towel, and coffee cups that seem to want to launch themselves off the edge of the porch at the slightest provocation (a slight problem with living in a house that bounces on a set of springs). For the most part, when something new comes in, something old goes out.

A few years ago, I splurged and got a new bed. The old bed—one I used for three years—was a gift from some friends in Portland just before I finished the little house and they left town. They had packed everything up, winnowed their stuff down to a small crate that was being shipped to Hawaii, and then wandered into their backyard to address what couldn't fit: ornamental bowling pins, yard art, picnic tables, and the like. In the end, I was asked to babysit a lawn chair and a giant grasshopper welded out of old lawn mower blades (art that was lighter and less bulky than the metal moose welded out of an old acetylene tank and bicycle parts). I figured the yard art would be easy enough to plant in the yard wherever I went. The lawn chair was more challenging, so I parked the metal foldy part in a friend's garage and kept the cushion to create a bed for my loft.

The lawn chair cushion worked fairly well. It had a low profile and was lightweight, so I could easily drag it up the ladder into the loft. I felt like a genius for improvising such a supreme bed: my blankets fit perfectly when I folded them in half, and there was plenty of room to fit me and my dog as long as she slept behind my knees and I slept on my side (which I normally do). For the first year or so, things were fine, but then things changed.

RooDee decided to park herself in the geographic center of the bed, never to the left or right, or down near my feet, or off on the exposed wood platform, but in the dead center of the bed. This left me sleeping like a tube sock on the thin side of the mattress, sleeping until I'd wake up and argue for space with my dog, hip-checking her, and groggily harrumphing around until I could fall back to sleep on my little cotton swab. I put up with this for a while, pacifying myself that I was still a rough-and-tumble adventurer, able to sleep on her backpack or make a pillow out of a wad of dry leaves shoved in a T-shirt. Surprisingly, the little mind game worked (I wasn't miserable, nor was I happy) until I woke up one morning with my ass crack on backward, as my brother once said; feeling like someone had hit me in the kidneys with a bowling ball, with a stiff lower back so painful that I had to crawl on my knees to put on my socks and shoes. So I broke down and decided to splurge on a new bed.

As a side note, I have to admit that I was also getting a lot of guff from my friends for "sleeping single in a single bed," as derided in a horrible '70s song. They were encouraging me to double up, "to get out there and live a little." "If you build it, they will come," my friends had promised, and then broke into peals of laughter.

So I found a local company to make a wool mattress for me, something a few inches thick and the size of a double bed, and easy to pull up into the loft or drag out for spring-cleaning. According to my research, wool was a perfect material: grown by local farmers on the backs of happy sheep, "eco-friendly, creating a micro climate that is restorative and practically medicinal," as it said in one ad. I was sold, and figured this was an awesome investment, even though it was hard to believe a mattress should cost four hundred dollars.

The wool mattress factory was on a farm just outside town, and as I drove down the gravel driveway, I was positively giddy. I couldn't wait to heft my normal-size mattress into the back of the truck and up into the loft.

I walked into the factory and asked about my mattress, exclaiming that this would be "the best bed ever" and "Man-o-man, isn't this a great factory," and a few minutes later a woman walked out of a back room holding a cardboard box the size of a baby chair. I was crushed, and stared at the box. My lips quivered and I almost cried.

"This is a wool topper, meant to slide over your mattress," the lady explained.

"But I don't have a mattress. I mean, I have a mattress but it is more like a seat cushion, and the word *cushion* is more of a suggestion than a reality."

She pulled out my paperwork and explained how I had purchased a topper. "It goes on TOP of the bed," she explained again, sandwiching her hands together and smiling.

I half smiled while holding back tears, and numbly walked back to the truck.

On the way home, I stopped at a store and bought a piece of memory foam. I hated doing this; I had inspected the factory where memory foam was made and had watched as giant loaves of the stuff squirted out the ass end of a machine, ballooning out of a series of pipes and chemical tanks into a pillow the length of a football field. From there, the mass was sliced like a loaf of bread into two-inch-thick mattresses that were wrapped in plastic, sealed, boxed, packaged, priced, and shipped all over the world.

"I thought my wool would be puffier," I told the memory foam salesclerk.

The saleslady nodded like she'd heard it all before, and I got in my truck and nearly cried. I hated my new bed.

When I got home, I pulled the foam out of its box and stretched it out on the back fence so it could bake in the sun and off-gas. It smelled a little funky, like the waiting room at the dentist's office, but not horrible. I sat in a lawn chair across from the foam and tried to make peace with it, and to imagine what people did in the old days when their back would crap out and the miracle of toluene diisocyanate, or TDI as they called it at the memory foam factory, didn't exist. I replayed the inspection that I had done at that factory, the way the chemical-tanks had emergency backups for the shutdowns, and turn-offs for any overflows. It was all very sophisticated, metered, measured . . . safe. And the end result was a soft and squishy wad of goo that, at this moment, even as it hung across the fence like a wet noodle, looked like the sort of thing that would help my back heal. "God," I mumbled, "I need a night of sleep!"

This was the sort of bargaining and reasoning that I did with myself more than a thousand items: the vehicle I drove to work, the wool rug in the great room, the propane I used to cook, pillows, Q-tips, toilet paper, coffee, the Christmas wreath I hung on the door, the shampoo I used, and food . . . bananas, beer, bread, asparagus in the middle of winter. All of my choices have been messy and inaccurate . . . and humbling beyond words.

As far as the bed went, a day after stretching the wad of polyurethane over the fence, I had a bed—a grown-up bed, with acres of luxurious padding that could be navigated by my dog and me, and a special someone if that ever happened.

And it did, and has. Just saying.

////////////////

All kinds of interesting things have come and gone in the little house: a taxidermy hawk, a small earthquake simulator, and that giant pair of red plastic clown shoes that I had previously sent to my friend Chinn but then she mailed back to me, explaining that she wanted me to wear them to her wedding as her maid of honor. I even had my own personal oxygen generator for a while.

The generator was prescribed by my doctor, and was designed to compensate for the way my heart was underperforming. I'd been feeling tired lately, like it was a monumental effort to collect my dog and drag her up to the loft and an epic feat to walk us around the block in the morning. The plan was to crank this thing on at night, slip a lovely plastic cannula around my ears and up my nose, and suck away on pure oxygen, with the end result being spunk, vim, and vigor.

I went to a medical supply place to pick up the generator and tubing. A lady gave me a short tutorial while I was signing several waivers, offering a gentle "I hope your patient does well" at the end of her speech. I gave her a look like I was swallowing the wheels off the generator, then the desk between us, and then the building that housed at least seven other desks. "Thanks," I offered, and turned to load the machine into the truck. A minute later, buckled up and a mile down the road, I sat at a stoplight and cried, glancing at the generator like a jailer who was marching me into solitary confinement.

Driving home, I remembered how Mark's oxygen generator had whirred away day and night, pumping air into his dwindling lungs and reminding all of us (but especially him) that he was dying. And now I was doing the same. Or was I?

I pulled the unit into my house and tucked it in a corner, where it looked overly large and awkward. That night, I dragged the plastic tubing into the loft, flipped on the machine, and then crawled off to bed with my dog. The machine puffed away, vibrating and echoing inside my tiny house, and the nasal cannula slowly baked the inside of my booger holes until they dried up and bled.

The next night, I shoved petroleum jelly in my nose and wore a pair of small foam earplugs, but the racket still drove me nuts until I crashed down the ladder, shoved the unit out on the porch, and slammed the front door behind it. This created a small plumbing issue, as I had to snake the tubing from the front porch up the side of the house and through the loft window, but it worked; I slept, smirking at my own resourcefulness.

A few days later, I started to notice that my legs and arms felt jingly in the morning. Maybe it was the oxygen, but I supposed it was more realistically the constant vibration created by the whirling generator sitting on the porch. My house doesn't sit on a foundation; there's nothing to dampen the sway of big wind in the eaves or the rattle of machinery tapping away on the trailer frame all night. So I grabbed the unit and shoved it under the house, placing it in the dry gap below the trailer and the grassy pad below. This seemed smart and required only an extra ten feet of plastic tubing, to run from below the house, up over the porch, across the siding, and through the loft window into my dried-up nose holes. Problem solved, and I actually slept a bit better.

A few weeks later, Rita asked how things were going with my "contraption," and I acknowledged that it was less than a luxurious step up at the Beverly Hotel à la Tiny House. She laughed at that and a few minutes later, when I set her dinner on the TV tray in front of her, she reached out and tapped my hand—a gentle swish-tap that reminded me she understood.

Rita was the one with problems. While she had adjusted over the years to her limited mobility, she still relied on a wheelchair, a walker, a cane, a wood gizmo to hold her cards when we played poker, and the help of an assistant every Thursday to give her a bath. She had it rough, compared to many, and then her vision started failing, too. As she would say: "Macular degeneration . . . never saw it coming."

My ability to talk with Rita was one thing—and it was fairly limited—but my desire to tell the neighbors why I had tubing laced around the front of my house was even further afield. So when the neighbor asked what kind of machinery I was running so feverishly through the night, if it was "the air compressor for your nail gun," I had deflected the question without much angst, offering: "Aw, geesh, you can hear that?"

This was where all my courage dried up—when I had a chance to divulge my big secret: "I have congestive heart failure and am using an oxygen generator because that's what sick people do, what weak and infirm people do as they try to string together longer, better days to spite shorter, more fucked-up expectations." But instead, I laughed and told the neighbor that I'd dampen the noise.

That night, I wheeled the generator into the garage and stretched a new forty-foot length of tubing across the lawn, up the front steps, past the front of the house, and into the loft window. Finally, all I could hear was the *pssst* of air puffing out of the cannula, my lungs expanding and contracting, and my heart lub-dubbing erratically. I rolled on my back and cried, letting the tears roll back into my ear holes around the nasal cannula. "This is what it has come to," I whispered. "What's next?" My dog butt-checked me and curled into my hip, sighing deeply and breathing slowly.

A few weeks later, I took the generator back to the medical supply store. "Did your patient expire?" the woman asked.

"No," I said, "not yet."

I'm still alive and well, and my heart condition hasn't lessened my desire for stuff. It's no easier to navigate the sea of "need" that I feel when I walk into Target (or any other box store) than it was when I lived in my big house. I want things. I want to buy the entire fifth season of *The West Wing*, a package with seven or eight DVDs and hours of mindless television entertainment. I want to buy a new hat and a turtleneck sweater that will hide the wattle jangling under my jaw, and I want to buy some cough syrup so I'll sleep through the night without waking up to the rain on the roof. But I won't do that, not today anyway.

My most recent purchase wasn't a gadget (like the six-inch drop hitch), but something functional: underwear. Powerful underwear.

I had been feeling fragile, like I needed a secret weapon to deflect the mounting sea of fear that I'd been feeling about my health. So I purchased two pairs of panties. One had a cartoon of Wonder Woman printed on the fabric, and the other (a blue pair with red ribbing) simply carried a giant S on the front. Superwoman.

The very next morning, I woke up to a pair of firemen pounding on Rita's back door. "Fire Department!" they yelled through the closed door.

I launched myself down the ladder and leapt into the backyard, wearing nothing but my Superwoman underwear and a T-shirt. The firefighters spun madly on their heels as I pounced out of what they thought was a toolshed sitting behind Rita's house. I gave them a stern, knowing look as I ran past them toward the front of the house.

In the front yard, a few more firefighters were standing at the front door, and they too spun around, surprised by the powerful lady in her powerful underwear, bearing down on the door. It was slow motion: me racing in, giving them a look like *Follow me!* and then unlocking the door to allow the firemen to stomp in on their own accord, as I charged through the house into Rita's bedroom. I found her on the floor, collapsed under the weight of her body.

"Jesus, Mary, and Joseph," she screamed. "Dee, help me! I'm sitting on a box of Kleenex!"

The firefighters clamored in with their regalia of suspendered fire pants, overly large boots, and muscular man bodies. One of them gave Rita a quick exam, and then helped her back into bed as I fluffed her pillow and rearranged her blankets.

Rita perked up, surrounded by five or six firefighters and me in my panties. All of us stared at her, and that's when we offered a collective sigh. Rita was okay. She had simply fallen out of bed and couldn't get up; problem solved, danger averted. And that's when I realized I was the odd man out, standing there in my undies. So I put my hands on my hips, framing the large S, and looked off toward a fake horizon. In a deep, booming voice, I said, "Well, I think my work here is done." Then I grabbed one of Rita's robes and thanked the firemen for their time.

Months later, I ran into one of those firefighters at the local pizza joint, who recognized me and laughed. "Oh my God, Superwoman, I've been telling that story all over town! How is Rita, anyway?"

Keeping the Peace

There are very few opportunities to discuss your underwear in public. That's what I told my friends Tammy and Logan as they finished setting their new tiny house in a friend's side yard, nearly six years to the day after me. Their yard was in Portland, and as part of the package, they shared a washing machine and dryer with the big-house owners, a situation that had led Tammy to question her panties decorated like a Christmas package with reindeer and ribbon. "It's all about getting comfortable," I laughed, and then we turned to Logan and asked about his skivvies.

When I first moved in, I felt bombarded by the way nothing was my own anymore; the night crept in at three or four in the morning, rolling past the window sill and cuddling into the airspace between me and my pillow, and the dog and my breath.

It settled in and took over, and the same was true with the sound of Keeva and her friends, late at night and sitting in the nearby sauna.

We had constructed the sauna earlier in the summer, using salvaged materials that included an old Franklin stove that my boss had dragged to the Pacific Northwest from Louisiana. That stove was well over a hundred years old, and it still managed to heat up our tiny sauna, tucked near the garage, in a corner of the yard only thirty feet from my house.

Keeva and her friends had heated themselves into sweaty mush balls, sitting in the sauna gabbing about this and that (all I could hear was the occasional brah-ha-ha of laughter). They heated themselves until they couldn't fathom another second in the tiny structure, and they exploded out the door, past the porch, and three steps into the snowy backyard, where they giggled and rolled in the snow like puppies.

All the while, I floated in and out of sleep, waking up long enough to hear one of the teenagers screaming that she had possibly frost-burned her "dant-ta-dant," which was followed by "Your *what*?" and more peals of laughter.

There wasn't any annoyance in that experience for me, even though I needed to get up early the next day and I wondered when I had become "the old lady in the nearby house," as I imagined Keeva could have easily described me to her friends (but she didn't . . . I was still just "Dee"). Those subtle (or not-so-subtle) interactions were the things that I missed when I was traveling. I missed being home, including the sound of Kellen practicing his cello, Hugh laughing with a friend in the driveway, Rita cranking *Jeopardy!* up to nine thousand decibels, and the way bats would ping into the backyard at dusk. All of that and more made living in the backyard a bit magical.

I wouldn't have it any other way, and so you might understand why I was freaked out when I learned that the city might want to put the kibosh on my situation. If they did, there would be no one to blame but myself. You see, a week earlier, an article about my house ran in the local paper, and someone (a complete stranger) had commented online, suggesting that I shouldn't be allowed to visit the public library because I wasn't paying property taxes while living in the backyard. The article only told the story of my house, and didn't mention the way I help Hugh and Annie, and the way they care for me; or the way I sometimes have to traipse over to Rita's house at two in the morning to move her box of Kleenex two inches closer to her, because they were out of reach and she needed them. No one wants to read about that kind of stuff in the paper, so this mean man (or woman) had assumed I was a squatter. In fact, he/she used that word just before explaining how people like me were undermining our economy.

So I had invited a city inspector to visit my house and see the backyard, and let me know what, if anything, was a problem. I didn't think anything was problematic, but I wanted to hear from them—a move similar to a foreman calling me at work, wanting to know if I could come by and see if there were any concerns with the way forklifts were moving spent solvent from one part of a building to another. In my experience, it was always better to be on the up-and-up than to be caught with your pants down.

Before that newspaper article, I hadn't ever thought about whether or not the city would have a problem with my living in an area formerly occupied by thatching ants; I never thought about it being a concern for the neighbors, the local fire department, or tax collectors.

The City Lady showed up at noon, and I showed her my solar panels, my compost toilet, and how I collected soapy water under the kitchen sink. She took photos of my cookstove and the outside of the house, and scribbled notes as we talked. I giggled at the way I treated her just like some factory foremen treated me when they offered me coffee and donuts. I offered her fresh strawberries from my garden, and complimented her on her blouse.

We had a short, reasonable exchange, but ultimately, this is what I learned: The city viewed my house like a travel trailer, and the code prohibited "living in trailers." So what was I supposed to do? There had to be a way around this.

My house was a hybrid, not quite a travel trailer or a regular house, and that made the city uncomfortable, not knowing which box to put it in. My house is also painfully small; it is nearly thirty times smaller than the average house in America, smaller than a parking spot, smaller than some SUVs, and smaller than the square footage of tissue provided by a roll of toilet paper. And yet, somehow, it still feels more like home than anywhere else I've ever lived.

I've lived in some odd places: in a woodshed behind my parents' house during a stint when I'd returned home from college and didn't want to go back. I've lived in a boat hut that was in a back pasture, alongside a lake that lapped up against the building foundation all through the night. I moved there just after I'd broken up with Rob, certain I'd find what I was missing by living with an axe and an outhouse, and ten thousand snow geese that would rise up off the lake when I'd throw open the door to pee in the middle of the night.

I lived in my van during graduate school while I was looking for a place to rent, and it was actually pretty fantastic except for the way I'd have to hop on my bike and ride up to the local McDonald's (sometimes pedaling at great speed) to use their bathroom first thing in the morning. And then there was the assortment of apartments and houses that my friends and I rented, where we lived without heat or hot water half the time. In one house, I had developed the habit of heating my body by holding my shirt like a net over the open flame on the oven; I did that repeatedly during the day, through the rainy winter, until one day, as I looked out the window, daydreaming, I sparked my shirt on fire. My housemate ran over and tackled me like an action figure, screaming, "DROP AND ROLL," as she barrel-hugged me and rolled us together across the kitchen floor.

So how could the city have a problem with my house? Was there a safety risk, or a problem with sanitation, human health, or the environment? Was it just a matter of keeping the peace, so the neighbors wouldn't imagine their property values plummeting because of the quaint view of the house "where the Keebler Elves likely slept"? (This was how a passerby once referred to my house, and after hearing that, I had yelled: "Simpler times, my friend, simpler times.")

There was more to it than the walls and the way the stove worked, the quarter-inch tongue in grooved knotty pine, the purple heartwood so dense it made my drill bit smoke as I was installing it along the loft rail. There was more here than the way it still smelled like cedar, and the way RooDee made a cave under the house behind the big bushes that I planted near the steps, and snored happily there all day long; it's bigger than the backyard and the fir tree, and the way I can drive down the alley, back in, and then reinstall those fence boards behind the house.

I wanted to tell the city inspector all about it, explain what I'd seen on the front porch at dawn and how the night before, Hugh, Annie, Keeva, Kellen, RooDee, and I had watched a movie outside on Rita's patio, circling our chairs around the tiny TV screen and DVD player, and laughing as quietly as possible after Rita went to bed. I wanted to say a lot but wasn't sure where to start; people don't want to hear about how your heart has melted into the dirt under your house, when all they want to do is take a few notes and get back to the office.

The inspector wrapped things up and thanked me for my time, in the same way I sometimes nod and say, "We'll be getting back to you with our findings." And sure enough, a few weeks later, Hugh and Annie got a letter from the city explaining how it was illegal to live in a travel trailer, but I could "recreate."

"Umm, are they talking about my house?" I'd asked Hugh as I held the letter in a shaky hand.

"We can fight this," he said. "March down there and make sure they understand you're not living like that."

"Like what?" I asked, starting to sweat.

"Like whatever"—he shrugged—"like everyone else who's walked into the backyard and seen there's something good here. This is good. Look, let's address this logically."

With that, we discussed our options: (1) I could formally "live" with Rita, but recreate in my house 99 percent of the time; (2) I could develop a petition and pay a fee to have my case heard before the city council; or (3) I could simply roll up the porch steps and find a place off in the woods far, far away from the city's watchful eyes.

Number 1 was out, because Rita and I would argue about whether or not various soaps were spicy or sugary in their scent; our cinnamon discussion already proved that. Number 2 was also out, because I couldn't fathom spending days and weeks closed up in a watery little office with the city council. I've spent enough time in a gray-colored cubicle, stamping paper and reviewing reports; I couldn't load more paperwork into the universe for someone else to process.

Number 3 was also out; I couldn't just snap my fingers and leave the backyard. I had spent too many hours sitting on the front porch at five in the morning, parked there with my legs crossed and my back against the front door, relaxing and pondering the fact that the sun had progressed like a miracle around the world overnight, the peas had grown another inch, and the clouds looked like an ad for air fresheners. Similarly, I knew Rita's evening routine, and what needed to happen if I volunteered to help her get into bed. It was like rolling a car off an assembly line, following a clear checklist of accomplishments: adult diaper changed and various balms and salves applied (check), robe and gate belt off (check), nightgown on (check), tissues (check), water glass (check), individual antacid tablets placed like easily accessed dominoes on the nightstand (check), lamp on, shoes off, nearby wheelchair parked close but not too close (check, check, and check).

I couldn't just walk away from everything I knew.

Realistically all the clean-cut options were out, leaving me with something in between, something a-legal: I would recreate in my house, as was appropriate for a recreational vehicle, which might include sleeping, eating, resting quietly, listening to music, hanging out, dressing, talking to myself, doing my taxes, and what not. I could define myself as Rita's caretaker— as a good neighbor who leaned just as heavily on her neighbors as they leaned on her.

This option seemed to fit how we regarded each other, and when I mentioned it to a friend, she told me that many cities have a special dispensation for caregivers; so people can recreate in their RV while they're helping their old mum with groceries, or perhaps setting up a hospital bed in the living room and sitting for hours at her bedside, resting their head on the metal hand rail and wondering what their mother is now dreaming.

It seemed to me, the city would likely support that sort of recreational living.

Broke Butt Mountain

When I was a girl, from time to time I'd help deliver calves on our family farm. It was always messy and sometimes sad, and always an enormous relief when it was over. We had a metal thing called "the puller" that we'd use in particularly hard deliveries. Essentially, it was a big metal chain with a couple of loop hooks on the ends and a hand ratchet in between. My dad would have my sister and me reach into the cow's uterus to find the calf's hooves. We'd pull those out if we could, then wrap them with a rag, and place them into the little hooks on one end of the puller. Then my dad, from what seemed to be a tidy distance, would ratchet out the calf like pulling a car out of a ditch, while my sister and I stretched apart the cow's labia and hoped for the best. It always ended with my sister and me covered in mucus and manure, sometimes happy with our new calf and sometimes crying as we helped our dad bury the stillborn calf. In any case, it was an enormous relief at the end.

I don't have much memory of the farm except for the messiness of it, and of course the noise of it—the way the cow during delivery would bellow, suck in, rattling her rib cage, and bellow again. I heard that noise again last year. The sound seemed to rise all around me, bubbling out of me, pouring out my nose and mouth, ear holes, asshole, pores, pads, palms, and hair follicles. I had fallen from the sleeping loft when the ladder dropped out from under me, a crazy freak accident that I couldn't have repeated even if I tried, and I wouldn't. I dropped seven feet, broke my sacrum and coccyx, and chipped my last lumbar vertebra. In a single second, I had effectively busted my ass and was reduced to nothing but a bellow. Keeva and Annie found me screaming with my eyes unfocused and rolled up into their sockets, just like the birthing cows. They called the ambulance, and before the paramedics arrived, they helped steady me and tried to persuade me to stop moving around (a bit of encouragement that I ignored) as I tried to change into clean underwear, just like my mother had taught.

I didn't go up to the sleeping loft for months, in part because I couldn't lift my left leg high enough to reach the steps—a strange and passing limitation. I slept at Rita's house for a week, and then once I went home, I found that I didn't have the courage to go to the loft or to pick up my dog like I used to; there was no bending down and hefting her up and carrying on like always.

During that time, people asked me what was next, often posing the question with the same steely tact my mother used when asking me about why I was cutting my own hair. I had no idea, really, except that I found myself sleeping on a lawn chair cushion on the floor in the living room. It was warm enough that I could sleep with the front door wide open, ten feet from my head, twelve feet from the spot where I saw a possum trying to drink water out of a glass I'd left on the porch. I slept like that for weeks, and in the morning I'd wake up to find my dog sleeping half in the house and half out, draped across the threshold like a doorstop. I can't tell you how much I appreciated that scene, or how it reminded me (like a surprise) that my house still fit me.

Still, sometimes I wonder if I'll live here till I die, till I am old and can't remember what my life could have been before. Will I always want to sit on the porch waiting for the sun to dry out my soggy disposition, waking me up to the reality of this place—this perfectly ordinary, exceptional life? Maybe. It turns out that the yard, the view, the rain on the roof, Hugh, Annie, and Rita are exactly what I want. Even the yuckier stuff, the gray days and long nights, are exactly what I want. Honest.

In late winter this year, I found myself staring out the window at the fir tree in the alley, leaning into my hand with my elbow on the table, exactly like a coffee commercial before the coffee is introduced and everything shifts from black-and-white into color. This is what I do when I'm avoiding putting on my raincoat and plunging myself into the grayness of winter, when I can't stand the idea of being cold (again) and walking around while my dog absorbs the rain like a cotton ball.

It was early February and it felt like the rain was trying to undo me, making my brain soggy and my complexion droopy, and reminding me that I live near the rain forest, where no amount of ultra-thick underwear could keep me from feeling damp because I *am* damp. I wondered if my dog was going through the same soggy-brained experience. She had recently taken to wanting to go out in the middle of the night and had even peed in the bed, something she had never done even when she was a puppy. So I'd started lugging her down the ladder at two or three in the morning. I'd open the front door and she'd hop down the steps in no particular hurry, like she didn't really have to pee after all. Sometimes I'd follow her out, stand on the porch, and watch her track right in the drizzly moonlight and then left, toward the garden, nose to the ground, and then simply stop, curl twice, and plop herself in the middle of the dried-up strawberries.

This behavior continued for months and it seemed to branch into other odd behavior: She would hide more and more in the thickets of the yard, concealing herself in the tall cool grass along the fence. She had a particularly clever hidey-hole constructed in the corner near the mailbox. You couldn't see her at all, hidden in the grass and low shrub, until the mailman would arrive and she'd launch herself out of the foliage like a lion on the great Saharan plains.

One day, after whistling my lips off and looking for RooDee in all the usual hideouts, I crawled on my hands and knees under my little house through an opening the size of a footstool. This was the secret door to RooDee's fort, the place where I'd seen her drag bones and where she'd go on hot days. So this was the basement of my house, a room I'd never entered. The area between the wheels and above the axles created a nice dry dirt floor with a fairly good expanse to crawl around, or if you were RooDee, you could stand up, stretch, chew on your butt, or do whatever else the day might involve. There was a secondary cave dug out under the front steps, a hollow that I never imagined as I'd wander up and down off the porch.

I looked around and relaxed a minute; it smelled like dirt and grass, and maybe just a little like dog spit and wet hair. I understood why RooDee had liked this secret little hidey-hole: it felt nicely contained, but also included a sneaky expansive view of the backyard past the front steps.

RooDee wasn't there, and I backed out slowly, laughing, and still wondering where the hell my dog had gone, and that's when I noticed her staring at me from the tall grass along the south fence. "What the heck, RooDee!"

Head tilt, tail wag: "What the what?"

It was like living with a spy. Someone who was constantly

watching you and taking expert notes, ready to present the facts on how you stayed up too late last night and didn't wash your hands after you peed the other day. Which wasn't all bad; it's good to be accountable to someone.

But then everything shifted.

Rita died. It was late April, a few months after RooDee started hiding in the yard and a day after an oxygen generator was dragged into her house by a good-looking guy who probably didn't need to work out at the gym anymore because the equipment was so fucking heavy. Rita died four days after I sat up with her one night, her feet dangling above the floor like she was a little girl, me rubbing her back like a tired mom who simultaneously wanted to help and also to roll into the blankets and fall back asleep. We chitchatted about the postcards pinned to the corkboard across from her bed, about the things that happened twenty years ago, ten years ago, and last Christmas, when her great-niece was in the desert, wearing a red bikini and a Santa hat. Rita died twelve hours after we talked by phone, and I explained how things were going in Portland, which was "great, and I'll see ya on Sunday whether you like it or not."

She died with Hugh (aka "Hughie Boodleheimer one-two-three," a nickname from when he was a little boy sitting in her lap as she read to him) holding her hand and leaning into her bed, with Annie and Kellen making their way in the early-morning dew across the yard toward her house; with me one hundred miles away, up and showered in Portland, busying myself to make a poofy spot on my hair lie flat, to look presentable, reasonable, and prepared for a day of teaching. Within a few minutes of Rita's death, Annie had called me to tell me about it. I imagined Rita lying there with Kellen resting his teenage hand on her shoulder. In the past year, Kellen's hands and feet, femurs, spine, and chin had grown exponentially— as if overnight, his body had shifted from the small eight-year-old boy who threw tennis balls at the garage for hours (and hours!) into that of a young man, a person capable of incredible kindness, listening when I cried at the dinner table one night, explaining that I was scared about my heart, that I was dying and I was afraid. At that moment, he had held my hand and rubbed my back (just like I had offered Rita). And now, there he was holding his dear great-aunt Rita, the matriarch who had helped raise him, who had allowed him to throw Nerf balls at her wheelchair as she rolled from the kitchen table to the living room lamp, daring her to toss the balls back as he ducked behind the couch. What was he thinking in those first few minutes? Was he safe and aware, and as shattered by reality as I was? I wondered about him as the phone static stretched the hundred-mile distance between Olympia and Portland—a thousand miles, ten thousand, the distance of the equator wrapped like a tight belt around the earth's waist . . . and then I burst into tears.

"There's no emergency here," Annie whispered into the phone. "Rita will be here when you get home. We love you."

I drove home twelve hours after Annie called, after teaching a workshop focused on tiny house building, and telling people about Rita, describing the time a few days earlier that she had wheeled into a furniture store for a new lift chair. She had dressed in her favorite skirt, a real piece of crap with the elastic totally blown out at the waist, and as she stood up from her wheelchair, and slowly turned on her heels, her skirt dropped to the floor. Without missing a beat, she casually said to Annie, "Well, there goes the skirt. But who cares? No one is around to notice." And with that, Annie looked up from her focus on Rita to see that the furniture store was packed with people: an entire family, clerks, a delivery guy, and assorted customers quickly averting their eyes from the train wreck near the lift chairs. Rita finished her turn and then sat her diapered butt on the lift chair, and she and Annie finally burst into laughter.

The class appreciated that story, and as I thought about it later while I was driving home, I sobbed. I cried on the highway from mile marker 2 in Vancouver, Washington, to mile marker 104 in Olympia. I didn't listen to the radio, or stop to pee, or try to play with my cell phone. Instead, I cried and wailed. At one point, perhaps out of exhaustion, I found myself surprised by the sound of my own crying; like a wounded animal—something unseen and moaning in the woods.

When I got home, I walked into Rita's house to find Hugh

and Annie and a small tribe of close friends. They were in various stages of noshing on snacks and crying and chatting about this and that to try to normalize things, having dropped whatever they were doing on a Saturday night to come over with food, beer, and wine.

RooDee ambled in and immediately leaned into one person after the other, gathering pats and accolades; this is what she always did. She'd meet folks as they walked down the driveway; if they were dog people, they'd lean down and pet her. If they were not, she'd give them their space and simply follow behind them as they walked.

After the meet and greet, we walked back to Rita's bedroom to see her. RooDee crouched low, like she was crawling under a fence; ears pulled back tight to her scalp, while swinging her head back and forth, sniffing the air. What did she sense that I couldn't? The room smelled like eucalyptus, roses, and beeswax. It was a strangely comforting smell, a kind, human smell just like Rita.

It was the weirdest thing watching RooDee; seeing how she regarded Rita's body and sniffed the floor, the bed and her body from the area near her head to her feet.

I sat down in a chair next to the body and RooDee parked herself at the foot of Rita's bed, curling into a tight ball and closing her eyes. She slept there for the rest of the night, and the following night too.

During the next couple of days, we all lounged about, slowly picking at our grief, including RooDee, who created a new hidey-hole just to the left of Rita's front door stoop. She would occasionally wander up to the back door and wag her tail, imagining that Rita would show up at any minute. She'd bark once and wag her tail (her normal routine with Rita, announcing that she would like another biscuit), but Rita wasn't there and so RooDee would slowly unwind her tail, drop it, and wander back to the front porch.

This continued for two weeks until RooDee died too.

I guessed maybe it was a broken heart, like she missed her routine with Rita even more than I did. RooDee missed how Rita would roll over to the back door to whistle, poorly (a pathetic *whoot whoot whoot*). If RooDee didn't respond, Rita continued by tapping on the glass door like a woodpecker, at which point RooDee would unearth herself from beneath the little house and wander over for yet another cookie or a plate of leftover mac and cheese.

I fell asleep in the backyard the day we took RooDee to the vet for cremation. I was listening to the hummingbirds buzz near the purple flowering plants in front of the little house; they seemed to have just now discovered the "bushes of unknown origin," as we called them, since we had no idea what they were. Everything was so normal and profoundly not normal at the same time; RooDee wasn't there. She wasn't sitting nearby, snapping at bugs who landed on her, frightening the birds, and Rita wasn't inside her house with the screen door open so I could hear her yell, "Rooooodaaaaeeee," followed by her really crappy attempt to whistle.

I fell asleep on RooDee's blanket and woke up with dog hair stuck to my upper lip like a crazy press-on mustache. So I went into Rita's kitchen to wash it off and drink a beer. Everyone was gone; Hugh, Annie, and Kellen were at a soccer game. Keeva was in Africa, and I was alone. I couldn't even watch TV—it was time for the six-o'clock news, but the TV cable got turned off when Rita died, so I couldn't watch Brian Williams, Mr. Weepy Eyes as Rita called him (a name he earned by looking like he was going to cry at any minute as he reported on the world's mayhem and missing goodness). So instead, I decided to drink my beer and mope around, and generally feel sorry for myself on this, my first day as an orphan.

///////////////////////

I am a creature of routine. Maybe most of us are . . . we wake up, hop in the shower, make a cup of coffee, make breakfast and a bit of lunch; we wake up our kids, kiss our spouse, and let the dog out for a pee. We go to work, punch a clock (even if it is metaphorical), and chip away at our day. And in the meantime, we come to know a little bit about the neighbors, the lady at the coffee stand, the bus driver, and the guy across the street who is probably running an illegal chop shop because he's up late at night with a torch, cutting up cars in his driveway (and even though I believe in freedom and the Declaration of

Independence, I am really annoyed by his tendency to use a ball-peen hammer at one in the morning). But even inside the stuff that bothers us, even inside the banality of so much of our day, we appreciate that everything is predictable and safe. Everything is clear, and you can navigate around the things that bother you and steer toward the things you love. And then someone dies and fucks the whole thing up.

Clearly, given my use of cuss words, I am mourning. Earlier, I'd thought about wearing black like Johnny Cash for the rest of my life. But everyone in the Pacific Northwest wears black—black raincoats, black hoodies, black jeans. And besides, black doesn't really describe how I feel; I am far more empty than full of tar. I feel like if I move too quickly, my shoulders will fall down and hit my kneecaps because the stuff in between is just air. So it is important that I sit very still in the backyard and do nothing, which causes me to notice there are a thousand different birds picking around at the fur that RooDee deposited in the strawberry patch. And it's easy to see that the day is perfect (not too hot and not too cold, and not raining or misting or threatening to move my pity party inside). RooDee would have loved this day just like every day, and likely wouldn't have put up with me moping around for long.

I wasn't just sad about losing Rita and RooDee themselves. I was grieving over every single pattern in my day-to-day that was now busted; how I couldn't figure out how to take a shower without asking someone (maybe Annie or Hugh) for permission to use Rita's bathroom. It was a habit, no less powerful than the way gravity can drop you to your knees.

There are two things I don't want to admit but will tell you as long as you pinky-swear not to tell anyone else and swear even bigger that you'll never ask me about them even if we become best friends who talk about everything. So here goes: The day after RooDee died, I crawled under the bench in my little house and curled into a ball the size of my four-year-old niece. Once I was shoved in there, I scream-cried into a down bootie that was sitting nearby, so no one would hear me and no one would have to know how deeply disturbed I was feeling. I kept my head down and hands over my head like a tornado was about to rip through my house (and it felt like that could happen at any moment), but it didn't and instead I ended up pulling a muscle in my abdomen, crying and blowing snot all over my down bootie. I cried like that for a half hour, and then the storm passed and I crawled out and drank some water like nothing had happened and I was normal again.

The second thing I did (and again, this is just between us) was punch the ceiling of my house very hard. I punched it five or six times while I was lying in the loft, crying about how the last time I had come to the loft everything was different. Rita was alive. RooDee was with me.

The few weeks since Rita had died, I had been sleeping downstairs because RooDee needed to get up a thousand times in the night, pacing around, shifting her weight trying to get comfortable, and I was afraid she'd launch herself off the sleeping platform so had started sleeping downstairs on a lawn chair cushion.

So there I was: comfortable in my "real" bed with the quilt that my mom made, and the skylight window over me showing how the moon really does sometimes look like a banana, which is funny and I would have said it out loud, and RooDee would have ignored me and instead would have sighed and scooted her butt farther into my knees. But RooDee was never going to do that again, so I punched the wood ceiling five or six times very hard while I cried.

I woke up in the morning with my knuckles scraped and bruised. Every time I reached for my coffee cup I felt embarrassed, ashamed at losing my shit in a way that included punching a four-thousand pound object. "Who does that?" I wondered.

Grief makes normal behavior a real pain in the neck, like the day after RooDee died and I went to get a pizza. I ran into a friend who asked, "How ya doing?" And I just stared at him, not sure how to respond: Should I go with "Okay and not," or maybe "Okay, and I feel like my heart is the size of a pebble, sitting at the bottom of a very deep, very dark well"?

"Great," I offered, smiling big, and wished him well, then raced back to my car.

Grief makes gravity heavier and air molecules denser, so

breathing is accomplished in a shallow, half-hearted way. The only nice thing—a helpful thing—was that I didn't have to go to work for a few days (my boss said it was okay, probably because her mom had died not too long before and she likely behaved illogically herself). I also liked the fact that I sat around in the backyard for several hours doing nothing: not mowing the grass or pulling out my tools to make something, not writing or drawing sketches of the little houses I'm designing for my friends. I didn't do anything but sit quietly and pay attention to the fact that my hollow chest was still beating. I was still alive and could see that the new normal wasn't so bad. In fact, it was quite beautiful . . . and that made me feel like the empty inside was just as full as the empty outside, which wasn't empty at all.

I took my crying and house punching to a therapist. She massaged arnica gel into my hand where the knuckles were bleeding and the big sandwich part was swollen, and told me she couldn't imagine anything so sad as losing Rita and RooDee. She was so kind and helped me fill out my tiny body a little bit more, so when I left, I didn't feel so much like a stick with a brain balanced on top.

Her ability to simply hold my hand even though I'd done an incredibly stupid thing (hiding under a bench and socking my house) was one of the kindest things ever.

That, and my friends Jenn and Kellie invited me to come

over and hang out with their boys. Harlan is four years old and one of the coolest kids on the planet (we had pinkeye together a few years ago and it bonded us) and his little brother, Andre, is about four months old (no pinkeye yet). At one point, Harlan threw a dozen or so freshly laundered socks across the kitchen floor, which was followed by us pretending he was a vacuum. He lay on his back, giggling, and I made vrooming sounds while pushing and pulling him across the floor to pick up the socks.

Maybe this was my new normal. I told Jenn and Kellie about punching the roof and Kellie reminded me that the Maori people bash their teeth in with a rock when they're grieving, an act that eliminates a lot of small talk and uncomfortable silences with strangers (everyone can see you're in a bad way and you don't have to suck it up and act normal, plus everyone likely has equally bad teeth, so you'd finally fit in). Maybe there wasn't any shame in simply taking a poke at my house or perhaps using a pillow if there was a next time.

I chased Harlan onto the couch and then pretended I didn't see him when I sat on him like a cushion. Then I pretended to fart on him and motioned like I was waving away a foul odor. And he thought that was one of the funniest things ever.

Later at home, lying in the loft alone and listening to the emptiness banging around the backyard, I cried some more. I cried lying on my left side, then my right, and then I opened the small window near my bed and cried while resting my head on the window jamb. It was exhausting work, and after a while

I realized I had quieted just enough to hear the tree frogs. And the port downtown was stewing away with any number of generators and forklifts and hustle and bustle, and whatever the hell else they do that sounds like a distant avalanche. This is what RooDee listened to, lying in the strawberry patch; what Rita got when she leaned out her bedroom windows; and now what I had, curled into the loft at midnight. Everything had changed and nothing at all—home was still the place we all fell asleep, even if some of us were missing.

One More Thing

In an hour, I'm supposed to get up in front of a couple dozen people and talk about how to build a little house. They've all paid money for this experience, perhaps borrowing from their children's college trust or skipping meals for months to pay the workshop fee, so you can understand why I'm nervous. I worry that they'll view me as flawed by the way I am walking with my toes balled up, holding the end of my flip-flop together with a wad of duct tape after my new, dear, sweet puppy, OluKai, chewed the crap out of it. She's done the same thing to the bottom of my shirt and my pillow; meanwhile, the nearby rawhide chew toys, dog bones, and stuffed toys sit untouched.

A few years ago, I started a company with a friend, geared toward helping other people build—helping them understand that life in a little house isn't necessarily simpler, but is layered with challenges that come in the oddest form. When I first moved into the backyard, I was reluctant to tell people where I lived, not because I thought it was illegal or amoral, but because I felt that they'd read something into it—they'd think I was broken and needed help, and was unable to live like a normal forty-year-old lady. I'm not sure when that little prejudice developed: thinking that people who live with others, long past their rabble-rousing youth, are shifty. It's like learning that the man you love still lives with his mom. It makes you ask questions. I'd ask questions too, but these days my questions are different.

I think I'm more curious than I used to be—curious about why people live like they do and how they make sense of their time. Do they have neighbors who are tracking their movements in such a way that they'd know just the right moment to rush in after they've fallen? Do they see how the sun has made it like a champion around the world overnight, and that all day today we get another chance to be brave, to exercise our humanity with boldness and deft precision, even if it's just in helping the old neighbor lady get her groceries into the house?

These are the questions I fold into our discussions of HTT tension ties, which I explain are "long metal brackets, capable of withstanding five hundred pounds per square inch of uplift." Something I normally get to say without limping with a wad of duct tape underfoot.

In the years since I built my house, I've talked with a lot of people who are curious about similar things. They want to access their inner carpenter, to challenge themselves to build their own home, and to develop an innate sensibility that allows them to know the difference among sticks of cedar, fir, and oak simply by the way they smell. More important, they want to examine their lives, and discover what makes them truly happy, which leads them to reconsider how they want to live within a community.

If I were to create a list of all the reasons Rita called me over to her house, it would probably look like the reason people hire a plumber or a professional caregiver: unclog the toilet, fix the kitchen sink, stare at the hot water heater to understand why it seems to be failing, remove the toilet in the bathroom so there's more room to maneuver a wheelchair, put it back; help pull up the adult diapers, dab ointment in the most sensitive, personal spots before the pull-up; talk about the adult personal spots with the same tone used for our discussion of the mailbox and how it needs to be repaired so it doesn't slouch in its position near the fence.

Rita responded to my needs too, offering a shower, a washing machine, and a large kitchen sink where I could rinse the giant bowl of strawberries I'd just harvested from the garden. But the plumbing exchange wasn't the reason our living arrangement worked; instead it was the way Rita and I would giggle at the commercials for Viagra that would blast into the living room while we were watching the evening news, and the way we would talk about Kellen's baseball game while I was refastening the Velcro on her shoes.

If more people understood how nice it is to have a sense of home that extends past our locked doors, past our neighbors' padlocks, to the local food co-op and library, the sidewalks busted up by old trees—if we all held home with longer arms— we'd live in a very different place. All over America, there'd be people living in the shadow of older people who know every word to the song "Fly Me to the Moon." There'd be more people attending middle-school talent shows and walking quickly with warm bowls of soup from one house to another, so as to enjoy an impromptu dinner with others.

We wouldn't feel so alone, no matter the size of our houses or our bank accounts, no matter whether we had good health or congestive heart failure. We would begin to see that each mo- ment presents an opportunity to relax, to notice that the wind has shifted and a storm is coming, or that our friend's toddler has decided to wear dinner instead of eating it. We would see that each minute counts for something timeless and, if we want, we all can find our way inside these big, tiny moments. That's my experience, anyway, and it seems to be what a lot of other people have found.

I've met lots of people who have decided to do something

similar: downscale out of their big house into a modest, almost too-tight abode, where windmilling unused stuff out the door is one of the most cathartic things they'd ever done. Some have even built tiny houses similar to mine, or they've modified RVs, buses, boats, and New York City studios. And the end result, according to what they've told me, is that living with less stuff offers a sense of happiness that they didn't even know they were missing; they discover that it's cool to have time to volunteer to refurbish the vacant lot a few blocks away into a playground for kids.

I love those stories. I was gobsmacked when Tammy and Logan told me they wanted to move out of their already tiny five-hundred-square-foot loft apartment to a little house like mine. Similarly, Kate, who lived in a small apartment in San Francisco, wanted to build her own house, diving into carpentry with very little experience but no less chutzpah than Amelia Earhart over the Atlantic Ocean in a small plane, and navigating (like I had) the difference between a floor joist and a roof rafter until she'd constructed a perfect little house. In Kate's case, she wanted to build a tiny house where she could come and go as she wanted, maybe hunkering on her parents' blueberry farm for some period of time, helping them with the harvest, and living elsewhere at other times. Si, the local beekeeper, also wanted to discover his inner carpenter. He worked slowly through the building process, designing a house that reflected his environmental ethic and a desire to live lightly on the planet. In every case, these people wanted a sense of home that included the people and natural environment around them, even if nature was nothing more exotic than the squirrels balancing on the telephone lines in a busy urban neighborhood.

For me, the idea of living small has always involved being curious—taking a look at how my day-to-day is connected to the larger world around me, and to the delicate universe that sits between my ears and in my small body. So at four or five in the morning, as I'm lounging around in the loft, I'll work on a list of things that I'm currently curious about—a list that I keep expanding and refining:

1. How many minutes can I abide the moon staring at me through the skylight?
2. What is the name of the bird that sounds like a broken shopping cart wobble-wheeling around the backyard so early in the morning?
3. How many people slept under the Fourth Avenue bridge last night? Were they safe, and are they in a place to get warm now that the sun is finally coming out?
4. What happened to the neighbor's cat?
5. How many minutes is the average kiss? How many hours have I spent kissing? Is it okay to break the

hours into minutes, seconds, moments, flashes—instants that carry just as much weight as the hour itself? Is it okay to apply the same logic to sitting on the beach at sunset; to listening to my sister laugh so hard she isn't making any noise, just wheezing a series of *zzzz-zzzz-zzzz* sounds; and to sitting with my three-year-old niece in my arms, watching her slowly fall asleep and then begin to drool?

6. How many other people are reclining like me, and staring at the exact same clouds forming and re-forming into what, just now, appears to be a car full of pickles?

7. Next time I'm online, research what Wikipedia has to say about the four-hundred-year-old tree that lives down the block. It looked like it was doing toe-touches into the neighbor's yard during the last wind storm. Also research: hawks that live in the median on the highway, dogs (non-chewing), clouds (all).

8. Whose idea was it that we should all get jobs, work faster, work better, race from place to place with our brains stewing on tweets, blogs, and sound bites, on must-see movies, must-do experiences, must-have gadgets, when in the end, all any of us will have is our simple beating heart, reaching up for the connection to whoever might be in the room or leaning into

our mattress as we draw our last breath. I hate to put
it in such dramatic terms, but it's kinda true.

On those days, I'll work on my list, thinking that then maybe I
can fall back to sleep, but instead, I toss—left side and right—
then lie flat on my back to stare at the knots in the wood ceiling.
I've been doing this for so long that now I've come to recognize
the knot patterns, and have made them into the eyes and nose,
ears and round heads of an assortment of cartoon characters.
This is the sort of imagination that develops after living with
your head a few feet from a beautiful knotty pine ceiling;
I've tried to explain this to would-be builders, so they can be
prepared.

Later, I'll grab OluKai (whom I've been calling "Oly" for
short) and amble down the ladder to start the day. I'll make
tea, get dressed, and try not to notice that Oly has eaten an
inch off my left pant cuff. And then I'll launch myself into the
backyard to start another day.

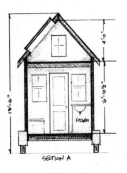

SECTION A

ACKNOWLEDGMENTS

I'd like to acknowledge the following people and entities. Without them, there really wouldn't be a book.

Paul Hawken, who inspired me to use words other than *tiny* and *big*, and to write absolutely from the heart. And to my friends and family, who have encouraged me and who haven't seemed to mind that I sometimes suddenly have to stop what I'm doing so I can jot down what they've just said, scribbling madly on a piece of paper—slips of paper they'll be happy to know are largely incomprehensible because I'm usually laughing too hard later to read my writing.

Many thanks to my editor, Sarah Hochman, at Blue Rider Press; David Fugate of Launch Books; and my co-conspirator at Portland Alternative Dwellings, Joan Grimm. And more thanks than there are sticks of wood in Oregon to Jenn Berney, who somehow was able to edit this book while raising two children, working a full-time job, making soup, chopping wood, running a marathon, and making me understand that anything is possible . . . even, crazy as it sounds, writing a book.

And finally, deep bows to Hugh, Annie, Keeva, and Kellen, who have created a sense of home with me that has retooled my heart and made me . . . Me! Many blessings.

One final note: The events I've written about are real, but I've massaged the timeline a bit to accommodate the story. If you want the long-winded, properly timed version of things, you'll have to take a road trip with me where we'll both confess everything out of boredom and proximity.